D. Caroline Coile, Ph.D.

Chihuahuas

Everything About Selection, Care,
Nutrition, Behavior, and Training

BARRON'S

D1410776

2 CONTENTS

The Collect of the Day

The Lord be with you.
And also with you.
Let us pray.

Almighty God, the fountain of all wisdom: Enlighten by your
Holy Spirit those who teach and those who learn, that,
rejoicing in the knowledge of your truth, they may worship
you and serve you from generation to generation; through
Jesus Christ our Lord, who lives and reigns with you and the
Holy Spirit, one God, for ever and ever. Amen.

The Lessons

A Reading (Lesson) from _____.

The Word of the Lord.
Thanks be to God.

AYE, CHIHUAHUA!

She's played the role of hot water bottle, religious sacrifice, main course, desert dweller, canine curio, cash crop, and lap guard. She's survived where others would have succumbed, and prospered when others would have perished. She's that **pequeño perro** *from south of the border—the Chihuahua.*

Considered one of the few breeds native to the Americas, the Chihuahua traces back to the early Olmec, Toltec, and Aztec civilizations of Central America and Mexico. How the Chihuahua originated, how it interacted with its people, and what became of its ancestors will remain the secret of the ancients. The history we have is cobbled together from artifacts, occasional writings, and conjecture. Some breed experts even theorize that the Chihuahua is actually of European or Asian origin. Regardless of its birthplace, the Chihuahua matured and prospered in the Americas, and will forever be identified with the land we now know as Mexico.

Of Toltecs and Techichis

The Olmecs of Central America probably developed the earliest Chihuahua-ish dog, which we know mostly from the carvings of the Olmecs' successors, the Toltecs. These Toltec carvings of the ninth century A.D. depict small plump dogs with a rounded head and erect ears, clearly reminiscent of Chihuahuas. They may have been raised as pets—that part is not clear—but they were primarily raised for their meat. The dogs, known as Techichis, were considered a delicacy to be enjoyed by the nobility on special occasions.

The Techichi is believed to be the ancestor of most Central American breeds. When the Aztecs conquered the Toltecs, they further developed the Techichi along with several distinct types of dogs. Their dogs served as sources of food and hair, as beasts of burden, and as sacrificial offerings. The Aztecs sought to ensure prosperity by appeasing their gods with ceremonial blood offerings, usually of captive humans. When humans weren't available, they sacrificed dogs, preferably the red or gray Techichis that lived in the temples of the priests.

But why dogs? Perhaps the answer lies in the associations between dogs, illness, and death that so many early cultures held. Many ancient people, including Aztecs, thought diseases could be transferred from ill people to dogs, thus curing the people. This belief probably arose from the dog's ability to function as a living hot water bottle; a little dog placed on an aching joint could make the pain go away.

The Aztecs took this belief a step further, and sometimes burned dogs along with the deceased in the belief that sins of the human would be thus transferred to the dog. A small red dog was believed to guide the soul of the deceased to Mictlan, the underworld kingdom of the dead, helping the soul to cross the waters flowing between this world and the next. Almost every Aztec household kept such a dog ready for internment along with any family member who should die. Archeologists have found Techichi remains or clay figurines in human graves throughout Mexico.

When Hernando Cortes arrived from Spain in the 1500s, his men described a small dog that the Indians used for food, for hunting small game, and as children's pets. The dogs were said to be well-loved. It was the Europeans who first called them Small Indian Dogs or Techichis. While small, it was still quite larger than today's Chihuahua. The Techichi remained in Mexican families until at least the early 1800s. Several were discovered in Mexican rebel leader Santa Ana's encampment when he was captured in 1836. Before then, there were even rumors that he kept a pack of them for spiritual protection in battle.

But the Techichi became increasingly rare, so that by the mid 1800s it was thought the dogs had disappeared. But in 1850, several very small dogs—some long-haired, some short-haired, and some even without hair—were discovered near the Mexican border state of Chihuahua. The long- and short-haired varieties were eventually dubbed Chihuahuas, and the hairless variety was dubbed the Mexican Hairless. In 1890, a boost to Chihuahua popularity occurred when one of that era's most renown singers, Madame Adelina Patti, was presented with a Chihuahua amongst a bouquet of flowers by the Mexican president. The Chihuahua became her constant touring companion as she traveled the world, exposing many people to her exotic dog.

Interest grew in the tiny dogs, but they remained very rare. Only in 1904 did the American Kennel Club (AKC) register its first Chihuahua; a total of five were registered that year. Soon afterward a small core of fanciers arose with the goal of perfecting and populariz-

ing this small, hardy dog; despite their efforts, the Chihuahua remained obscure.

Rise in Popularity

Like Adelina Patti, Xavier Cugat was a celebrity when he added a Chihuahua to his persona. The rumba king, as he was known, appeared with his Chihuahuas in movies and on television in the late 1930s and early 1940s. That's all it took. Once the public got a glimpse of these Latin lovers, the Chihuahua began one of the most meteoric rises in numbers of any breed in American Kennel Club history. The Chihuahua's popularity reached its peak in 1964, when it was the third most popular breed in the United States. Roughly a century after their discovery, the Chihuahua is one of the most recognizable breeds ever, and the AKC now registers tens of thousands Chihuahuas each year. Today both long- and short-coated Chihuahuas grace homes and laps around the world.

Chihuahua Charms

For many people there is no choice: The Chihuahua is the only dog for them. But even Chihuahuas aren't for everyone. Are you up to the Chihuahua challenge?

Size

The Chihuahua's small size certainly makes it convenient; it doesn't take up much space, its food bills are low, its grooming is a snap, and its exercise needs can be met at home.

But small dogs have drawbacks:

✔ They don't make effective protection dogs or great hiking companions.

✔ They run underfoot and can trip people.

✔ They can be injured by falling objects, larger dogs, wild animals, and wild children.

✔ They are more susceptible to cold weather, missed meals, and to certain health problems not seen in larger dogs (see page 9).

Chihuahua owners must be vigilant. Chihuahuas are not a good choice for homes filled with undomesticated children or lead-footed adults. Chihuahuas cannot live outside. They need companionship, they fall prey to larger animals, and they cannot withstand cold weather. Small dogs have a greater surface area, over which they lose heat, compared to their body volume, in which they generate heat, which means they lose heat more rapidly than do large dogs. Even long-coat Chihuahuas cannot cope with cold weather. Chihuahuas are tough, hardy, dogs—but not superdogs. They are little, they get hurt, and they get cold.

Temperament

Chihuahuas are intelligent, attentive, and willing to please, a combination that makes for trustworthy companions. They are one-family, even one-person, dogs, and can be devoted to the point of being clingy. Don't get a Chihuahua if you don't want an extra five pounds of love in your lap all the time!

But the Chihuahua is no "sissy" lapdog. Saucy, bold, and quick witted, Chihuahuas also make active companions and even protectors—sort of. Woe to any intruder's ankles who dares trespass without the resident Chihuahua's approval! It's important that young Chihuahuas are exposed to visitors at an early age so they learn to accept them graciously. Some Chihuahuas make up for their diminutive dimensions by making liberal use of their barking ability, a trait not always appreciated by neighbors.

Chihuahuas tend to be clannish, bonding closely with Chihuahua housemates and packing together to protect their territory against canine interlopers. Again, it's important that young Chihuahuas learn that non-Chihuahuas are not giant mutant dogs from Mars, but simply overgrown cousins.

Chihuahuas are among the most devoted of all dogs. They bond deeply with their family, becoming at once protective of them and dependent on them. They form a lifelong commitment to their people; unfortunately, too many people don't share that commitment. When the dog becomes inconvenient or loses its novelty, they send their trusting family

member packing. Being uprooted from loved ones is difficult enough for any dog; it can be devastating for a Chihuahua. Don't get a Chihuahua unless you plan on having her for life.

Health and Longevity

Chihuahuas are among the longest lived of dog breeds, averaging a life span of 13 years, with many living into their late teens. Most Chihuahuas are healthy throughout their lives, but no breed of dog is without conformation-related or hereditary health disorders, and the Chihuahua is no exception. Like many small breeds, Chihuahuas are prone to patellar luxation, a painful condition in which the kneecap slips in and out of position (page 82). Some Chihuahuas, especially older and fatter ones, are prone to a collapsed trachea (page 82). Hypoglycemia (page 83) can be a significant problem in puppies and some small adults. Other hereditary problems (page 82) occasionally crop up, but none is particularly prevalent in the breed.

Tiny dogs present some physiological challenges. It is difficult to reduce size proportionally in all parts of an animal, including its organs; for example, the eyes of small dogs are proportionally larger than those of large dogs. Very small dogs don't have the ability to store energy that larger dogs have and may succumb to the effects of food deprivation or minor illnesses that would scarcely bother a larger dog. It's actually a wonder that a breed that has been bred down in size to the extent the Chihuahua has is among the healthiest of popular breeds.

Sharing your life and home with anyone—dog or human—has its good and bad points. The good points of life with a Chihuahua are very good: A Chihuahua can be your pocket-sized protector and amiable amigo who can make any mundane task into an adventure. The bad points are the midnight walks in the rain, the soiled floors, the lack of freedom, the expenses, such as food, equipment, boarding, and veterinary, and ultimately, the grief of parting after a long life. Make the best of your time together. Start by choosing the best Chihuahua for you.

Choosing the Chihuahua was the easy part. Choosing a particular Chihuahua is the fun part. Saying "No" to the rest of them is the impossible part!

The Best Chihuahua for You

All Chihuahuas are special, but some are more special than others, or at least, more suited to you than others. You can find a Chihuahua with very little effort. You cannot, however, find the perfect Chihuahua so easily. When you look at prospective canine companions, consider three Chihuahua traits that drew you to the breed: Its good looks, its good temperament, and its good health.

Good Looks

You want your Chihuahua to look like a Chihuahua, which means she should be a tiny dog with a fairly stocky build. The Chihuahua head is distinctly rounded, and its muzzle short without being squashed in. Its ears stand erect, although they start out floppy. Its eyes are large. The Chihuahua standard of perfection (see page 90) outlines more particular requirements of Chihuahuaness; however, you don't need to be that picky unless you wish to show or breed your dog.

The appearance of the sire and dam of the litter is the best predictor of the looks of their offspring. Good breeders will have photos of the entire family available. By examining the pedigree for conformation champions (they have the letters "Ch" before their names), you can also get an idea of how well your dog's ancestors conform to the official standards.

Good Temperament

The proper Chihuahua temperament is "alert, with terrierlike qualities" according to the AKC standard. The Chihuahua has earned its position as one of the most popular breeds partly because of its stable temperament.

You should still take some precautions when choosing your future partner. Again, the personality of the sire and dam are the best predictors of their offspring's. Chihuahuas are naturally reserved with strangers, but they should not act afraid or aggressive. A dam with very young puppies may act protectively; if so, she should be revisited when the pups are a little older. Obedience or agility titles (these are letters such as CD, CDX, UD, MAX, or countless other agility titles, all placed just after the dog's name or even better,

Good Health

A good guide to the health of your prospective Chihuahua is the health of her ancestors. How old have her relatives lived to be? Are veterinary certifications of health clearances, such as heart, eye, and especially, patella certifications, available? The Chihuahua Club of America suggests that breeding stock be examined for heart defects, eye problems, and knee problems (patellar luxation). Dogs who undergo the required testing (if the breeders register the results) are listed with the Canine Health Information Network (*www.caninehealth.org*). A breeder whose dogs are listed here is probably one who tries to produce healthy dogs. Breeders can't predict or prevent every disease. But they can try, and in so doing, give you the best chance of sharing a long and active life with your friend.

Check out pages 82–83 for a description of some problems Chihuahua breeders and buyers should know about.

OTCH—obeience trial champion or MACH—master agility champion—before the name) in the pedigree indicate not only obedient ancestors, but also breeders who care about temperament.

Equally important is the environment in which the puppy is raised. Pups raised with minimal or aversive human contact during their critical period of development (from about six to ten weeks of age) may have some lifetime personality problems. That is why it is important that your pup is raised in a home, not in a garage, a cage out back, or a mass-production puppy farm. You want your Chihuahua to live as a housedog and companion; shouldn't she be raised that way?

Little Things

Chihuahuas with good looks, good temperament, and good health can still vary in many ways. What Chihuahua really makes your heart race?

Size

What's there to choose? Chihuahuas are little, period. According to the AKC standard (page 90) they should not exceed 6 pounds (2.7 kg). But in real life, they do. Some Chihuahuas have decidedly nondiminutive dimensions. They may weigh in at 10 pounds (4.5 kg) or more. Some Chihuahuas are longer legged and lighter boned than that described as ideal in the

standard. Their muzzles tend to be longer, and they have a more "deerlike" look, giving rise to the unofficial label of *deer type* Chihuahua. But a larger or leggier Chihuahua has some advantages as a pet. It is a better walking companion, and may fare better in obedience trials or be somewhat more immune to injuries or hypoglycemia. If you want a "true" Chihuahua that you can show or breed, then you need to get one within the standard. If you want a "true" Chihuahua you can love, get whatever one you want.

Some other Chihuahuas are at the lower end of the size scale, weighing in at 2 pounds (.90 kg) or so. Unofficially dubbed "teacup" or "pocket" Chihuahuas by some, they are not a separate type of Chihuahua but simply unusually small individuals. Most breeders advise that only experienced Chihuahua owners raise these dogs, as they are somewhat more fragile and vulnerable to conditions such as hypoglycemia. The tiny females are too small to breed safely.

Most experienced breeders advise that a Chihuahua at the upper end of the standard's limit—that is, one weighing 4 to 6 pounds (1.8–2.7 kg)—is ideal for a pet owner who wants an active and healthy companion that still retains its true Chihuahua looks.

Coat

Chihuahuas come in two coat types: the more familiar smooth coat, and the less familiar long coat. Neither coat type is difficult to care for. Both types can be born within the same litter. The smooth coat is the result of a single dominant gene. The long coat is not thick and requires only brushing a couple of times a week. Neither sheds a lot, perhaps because there is so little body area from which to shed!

Color

The palette of Chihuahua colors has something for everybody. Chihuahuas can be solid colored or parti-colored (spotted). The color pattern on either can be clear, sabled (dark-tipped hairs), masked, or brindled (color broken up by irregular vertical dark stripes). The color hue can be basically black or its diluted shades of chocolate or blue (gray), or red or its diluted shades of gold or cream, or white.

Thus, a Chihuahua might be a parti-color blue brindle—a white dog with patches of dilute

black (light gray) with darker gray stripes. It could also be a solid fawn, which would be a dilute red with no brindling or white spotting. Visit a large Chihuahua gathering and enjoy all the combinations before choosing a favorite. But one warning: You may decide that you have to have one of each, and that's a passel of puppies!

Sex

The differences between male and female Chihuahuas are slight compared to those in most breeds. Females tend to be smaller than males, but there's a great deal of overlap, and besides, what's the difference between a tiny Chihuahua and a teensy one?

Both males and females tend to get along well with one another. Males may be slightly sweeter, but some may think nothing of repeatedly lifting their leg on your furniture to mark

your house as their territory. On the other hand, females come in estrus ("season" or "heat") twice a year; this lasts for three weeks, during which time you must shield your temptress from amorous neighborhood males who consider your house a singles bar. You must also contend with her bloody discharge and possible attempts to elope with her suitors. The solution for both sexes is neutering (see page 68).

Age

Most people think of a puppy when they consider getting a new dog, but puppies aren't for everyone. True, they're cute and fun, but they're also an incredible amount of work. Chihuahua puppies are more fragile than larger breeds, and can succumb to hypoglycemia (see page 80) if they miss a meal or if they overexert themselves without sufficient nourishment.

Adults

Don't forget adult Chihuahuas. Breeders may have adult dogs available that would relish the chance to live as pampered pets. Chihuahua rescue groups (page 93) find homes for Chihuahuas that have fallen upon hard times; their former owners may have died, moved, or simply been unprepared to cope with the responsibility of dog ownership. These dogs range in age from young pups to geriatric seniors. The adult Chihuahua bonds surprisingly quickly to a new family; after all, they know a good thing when they see it!

Taking charge of a puppy means taking on extra responsibility along with the extra fun.

Many Chihuahua breeders elect to place only older puppies, preferring not to send a Chihuahua pup to a new home until the pup reaches 10 weeks of age and waiting longer for especially tiny pups. A breeder who is willing to take on this extra work to ensure that your puppy will be as strong as possible when she goes home with you is a breeder worth waiting for. However, this is only a good idea if the breeder can take the extra time needed to socialize the puppy during these critical socialization weeks.

Quality

Dogs are generally graded as pet, show, and breeding quality.

A pet-quality dog has some cosmetic flaw that would prevent her from winning in the conformation ring, but still has good health and temperament. Most such flaws would never be noticeable to the untrained eye. Perhaps she is a little too big, or her muzzle is too pointed, or the angles in her legs aren't just right. Big deal. A Chihuahua with a health concern such as patellar luxation might also be considered pet quality, but the breeder should thoroughly inform the buyer about the future consequences of any such problem.

Show-quality dogs should first of all be pet quality; that is, they should have good temperament and health. In addition, they should portray the attributes called for in the breed standard in such a way that they could reasonably be expected to become conformation champions in the show ring.

Breeding-quality dogs come from impeccable backgrounds, and are of even higher quality than are show-quality dogs. Breeding

CHECKLIST

Selecting Your Pup

Your prospective puppy should

1. have its first vaccinations and deworming.
2. be outgoing and active. Avoid a puppy that is fearful or aggressive. If a pup is apathetic or sleepy, it could be that she just ate, but it could also be a sign of sickness.
3. be clean, with no missing hair, crusted or reddened skin, or signs of parasites. Eyes, ears, and nose should be free of discharge.
4. have pink gums; pale gums may indicate anemia.
5. have no indication of redness or irritation around the anus.
6. not be coughing, sneezing, or vomiting.
7. not be thin or potbellied.
8. not be dehydrated, which can suggest repeated vomiting or diarrhea. Test for dehydration by picking up a fold of skin and releasing it. The skin should pop back into place.
9. have two testicles in the scrotum (if male).

The better quality you demand, the longer your search will take. A couple of months is a reasonable time to spend looking for a pet puppy, a couple of years for a breeding-quality dog. Begin your search for a high-quality Chihuahua by seeing as many Chihuahuas as possible, talking to Chihuahua breeders, joining Chihuahua Internet lists, attending Chihuahua competitions, and reading Chihuahua publications (see page 93). The Chihuahua Club of America is a good source for locating serious breeders as well as rescue prospects.

Sources

Most people seeking a Chihuahua look in all the wrong places to find their right dog. That's because so many people breed Chihuahuas with the goal of making money rather than producing healthy companions. Committed Chihuahua breeders do just the opposite;

quality means more than the ability to impregnate or conceive, but far too often these are the only criteria applied to prospective parents by owners unduly impressed by a registration certificate. It is difficult to pick a show-quality puppy at an early age; it is impossible to pick a breeding-quality puppy.

they make personal sacrifices in order to produce the best Chihuahuas available. They prove their dogs in some form of competition or therapy work, and screen them for hereditary health problems. Despite their best efforts, not every pup turns out to be competition quality. These pet-quality pups still have profited from the breeder's knowledge of genetics and puppy care, and still need good homes. Good breeders will screen prospective pet homes and will expect you to keep them abreast of your pup's progress and problems throughout its life. A good place to find reputable breeders is through the Chihuahua Club of America breeder directory online (*www.chihuahuaclubofamerica.com*).

Good Breeders

You can usually identify good breeders because they:

✔ breed only one or perhaps two different breeds of dogs. Most dedicated breeders spend years studying one breed and could never have the resources to do justice to several breeds. Multibreed breeders are too often small-scale puppy mills.

✔ breed no more than three or four litters per year.

✔ can compare their dogs to the Chihuahua standard.

✔ can discuss Chihuahua health concerns in general, and provide evidence of the health of their dogs. See pages 73–82 for a discussion of health concerns.

✔ have clean facilities that promote human and canine interaction.

✔ question you about your prior experience with dogs, your facilities, and your intentions regarding your new dog.

✔ discourage you from breeding. In fact, most good breeders will sell pet puppies only with an AKC limited registration, which means if they are bred their offspring cannot be registered.

✔ insist upon taking the dog back at any time in its life should you not be able to keep it. Good breeders care about the welfare of the dog for its entire life, not just until it walks out the door.

Rescue Chihuahuas

Be wary of a breeder who cannot meet these minimal requirements. The one exception is if you are looking for a rescue Chihuahua. Rescue Chihuahuas come from a variety of backgrounds. Some can be found in your local animal shelter; others may be in foster homes as part of various Chihuahua rescue organizations. A list of Chihuahua rescue contracts can be found at the Chihuahua Club of America's website at *www.chihuahuaclubofamerica.com*. Most of the dogs in rescue probably did not originate from conscientious breeders; if they had, their breeders would have taken them back when their owners no longer wanted them. That doesn't mean they make any less wonderful companions; it just means they need you even more.

TIP

Many small registries have sprung up to register dogs that don't qualify for AKC registration. The legitimate registrars in North America for Chihuahuas are the American Kennel Club, United Kennel Club, Candadian Kennel Club, and Federacion Canofila Mexicana.

How Much Is That Doggy?

Good Chihuahuas are not cheap. Good pet-quality Chihuahuas start at $750; show quality average $1,500. If that seems like a lot for such a little dog, remember, dogs aren't priced by the pound! Small dogs are expensive to raise. They often require Caesarean sections for birthing, and usually have small litters. Their veterinary bills, health clearances, and show expenses are the same as those of large dogs. Because they cost the same to produce, and are equally qualified for their major job—companionship—many breeders charge the same for pet and show puppies. Compared to the many years of companionship a healthy dog will bring you, a good-quality Chihuahua is the deal of a lifetime!

If money is a problem, consider adopting a rescue Chihuahua; they aren't cheap, either—after all, people tend to devalue items, including dogs, they don't pay much for—but if you offer an ideal home you may be able to foster dogs in need and work out an arrangement that helps everyone involved.

Registration

Don't think that the letters "AKC" will magically guarantee a good-quality Chihuahua. Remember, the AKC registers many thousands of Chihuahuas each year. AKC registration means only that the dog's parents were also AKC-registered.

Because of their popularity and the ease of keeping huge numbers for breeding operations, Chihuahuas seem particularly vulnerable to being exploited and foolishly bred. Chihuahua puppies are sold at flea markets, through puppy mills, and in thousands of backyard pens throughout the country. They are bred by people who never heard of testing for hereditary health problems, don't know about prenatal care and puppy socialization, and couldn't care less about the Chihuahua standard. Yet they all carry the AKC-registered insignia. AKC registration is a starting point, not a stamp of approval.

Registered puppies should come with a pedigree and either a litter registration certificate, individual registration certificate, or statement in writing clearly stating why such documents are not being supplied. The registration materials should already be available by the time the puppy is ready to leave for its new home.

They say you can choose your friends, but you can't choose your family. That's not true! Choosing your new Chihuahua will give you the chance to choose your newest friend and family member. So make the most of it.

THE LAP OF LUXURY

Congratulations! You're expecting! Channel your excitement now to make sure everything is perfect for your little bouncing bundle of bow-wow.

The Chihuahua Chalet

You want your new family member to feel at home, but you want your home to survive your new family member. So you need to make some plans before you bring your puppy home. Make some of your home off-limits at first. It's easier to allow your pup more free reign as she ages than it is to suddenly no longer allow her where she once could go.

What about furniture? Chihuahuas enjoy surveying their household while perched up high, but they can hurt themselves jumping off high places. In general, if they can't jump up to a place by themselves, they shouldn't jump down from that place. This rule is even more important for puppies and old dogs. You can make a ramp that leads to favorite lookouts or nesting spots. Even so, be careful that a sleeping Chi can't accidentally roll off a high bed. Also be careful that a sleeping person doesn't accidentally roll onto a helpless Chihuahua!

Puppy Paraphernalia

Furnishing your home with Chihuahua "stuff" is the next step toward making your house her home. The best sources for supplies are large pet stores, dog shows, and discount pet catalogs. Consider these for your shopping cart:

✔ Toys, toys, toys: Fleece-type toys, balls, stuffed animals, empty plastic soda bottles, and interactive toys that make the dog work to receive a treat. Make sure no parts of toys, including squeakers or plastic eyes, can be pulled off and swallowed.

✔ Chewbones: The equivalent of a teething ring for babies.

✔ Food and water bowls: Avoid plastic, which can cause allergic reactions in some dogs.

✔ Food: Start with the same food the pup is currently eating.

✔ Soft buckle collar: A cat collar may work well.

✔ Harness: A good alternative for a collar.

✔ Lightweight leash: An adjustable show lead is good for puppies.

✔ Sweater or coat for cold weather.

✔ Soft brush.

✔ Dog shampoo (see page 51 for choices).

✔ Nail clippers: guillotine type is easier to use.

✔ First aid kit (see page 76 for contents).
✔ Dog bed.
✔ Crate.
✔ Baby gate(s): Better than a closed door for placing parts of your home off-limits. Do not use the accordion-style gates, which can close on a dog's neck.
✔ X-pen or playpen.
✔ Fenced outdoor area.
✔ Doggy door.
✔ Poop scoop: Two-piece rake type is best for grass.
✔ Canine litter box and canine litter.

The Crate

Many new dog owners are initially appalled at the idea of putting their pet in a crate as though it were some wild beast. At times, though, your Chihuahua pup *is* a wild beast, and a crate is one way to save your home and sanity. A crate can also provide a quiet haven for your youngster. Your pup needs a place she can call her own, a place she can seek out for

rest and solitude. Place the crate in a corner of a quiet room, but not too far from the rest of the family. Put the pup in the crate on a soft blanket when she begins to fall asleep, and she will become accustomed to using it as her bed. If you have more than one dog, feeding in a crate can ensure that nobody steals somebody else's dinner. Used properly, your Chihuahua will come to think of her crate not as a way to keep herself in, but as a way to keep others out!

Note: The crate is a bed, not a prison. Leaving your dog in a crate all day, every day, while you are at work is unfair and can also lead to behavior problems. Locking an active, inquisitive Chihuahua in a crate without stimulation for too long can cause such frustration and anxiety that the dog will resent the crate. A crate should be the canine equivalent of a toddler's crib. It is a place for naptime, a place where you can leave your pup without fear of her hurting herself or your home. It is not a place for punishment, nor is it a storage box for your dog when you're through playing with her.

The X-pen

An exercise pen (or X-pen) is a transportable wire folding playpen for dogs. X-pens are helpful when you must be gone for a long time, because the pup can relieve herself in a doggy litter box in one corner, sleep on a soft bed in the other, and frolic with her toys—all in a safe, confined space. It's like having a little yard indoors. The X-pen provides a safe time-out area when you just need some quiet time for yourself, but before leaving your pup in an X-pen, make sure that she cannot climb out. Tops are available for incorrigible escapees. If you use an X-pen, cover the floor beneath it with thick plastic (an old shower curtain works well) and then add towels or washable rugs for traction and absorbency. Again, do not expect to stick your Chihuahua in an X-pen all day, every day and still have a sane dog.

The Fence

The number one Chihuahua accessory and lifesaver is a securely fenced yard. You may think that a little Chihuahua can't wander far, but she can wander far enough to be attacked by another loose dog, hit by a car, poisoned by a neighbor's carelessly stored chemicals, stolen by an opportunist, or lost in an over-sized world. You don't need a huge yard, just a handy and secure one. Ideally it should be available through your back door or a doggy door. Invisible fences are not usually a good idea for Chihuahuas because they still allow loose dogs to come on your property. Tying a Chihuahua out is similarly dangerous; she can-not avoid stray dogs and she can also strangle.

Chihuahuas have some special concerns when it comes to backyard safety. Puppies are so tiny that they can literally be carried away by some birds of prey and easily killed by some terrestrial predators. Don't leave a Chihuahua outdoors without supervision, and if you're in an area with wildlife make sure your fence keeps them out. In some areas, a covered run may be the only safe outdoor place for your dog.

Puppy-proofing

Puppy-proofing your home will be a lot easier if you do it before your new puppy is underfoot undoing everything as fast as you do it. You need to Chihuahua-proof your home just as you would baby-proof your home, but you need to do more than you would for a baby. Remember,

TIP

Identification

What would happen if your Chihuahua were lost? The best way to ensure your reunion is with identification.

✔ A license tag is one good means of ID, but large tags can get caught on branches and even playmates' teeth.

✔ A tag made of a brass plate fit snug to the collar is better; but collars can come off and dogs aren't always wearing them when they're lost.

✔ A microchip is essential. It's about the size of a grain of rice; your veterinarian injects it just over the dog's shoulders. Veterinarians and shelters have special readers that they pass over the dog to read the owner's information from the chip. Be sure to register the number.

Nobody plans to lose a dog; but those who plan ahead have a better chance of finding one.

your Chihuahua baby can tunnel like a mole, gnaw like a beaver, and run like a bunny—and she can do it all from a vantage point of six inches off the ground. Get down at her level and see what temptations beckon.

✔ Puppies can chew electrical cords and lick outlets, causing electrocution and burns. Puppies can also pull electrical appliances down on themselves by pulling on cords.

✔ Puppies can jump on unstable objects, such as bookcases, and bring them crashing down on themselves.

✔ Puppies can jump or fall from decks and staircases. Use baby gates, X-pen panels, temporary plastic fencing, or even chicken wire if needed in dangerous areas.

✔ Puppies can be crushed by slamming house or car doors, strangled in swinging doors, injured running into clear glass doors, and lost running out of open doors leading to unfenced areas. Use doorstops, screen doors, glass door decals, and extraordinary care to avoid these dangers.

Your puppy will naturally want to explore every niche of your home you never even knew existed, and she will do so by testing their strength with her teeth. You never know when something will be tasty! Chewed items left in her wake are your fault, not hers—you're the

TIP

Household Killers

✔ Drugs
✔ Chocolate (especially baker's chocolate)
✔ Rodent, snail, and insect baits
✔ Antifreeze
✔ Household cleaners
✔ Paint thinner
✔ Toilet fresheners
✔ Nuts, bolts, pennies, and any metal—especially zinc
✔ Pins and needles, and anything in a sewing basket
✔ Chicken bones or any bone that could be swallowed
✔ Sponges

one who should have known better. So if you come across one of your cherished items chewed to bits and feel compelled to lash out, go ahead: Hit yourself in the head a few times for slipping up. It may teach you a lesson—but such harsh corrections won't teach your puppy anything except that you are a mean ogre. A tap on the nose along with a firm "No," and then substituting the mangled item with a legally chewable item is more effective for convincing her to chew selectively. But the main responsibility is yours—surely you are more responsible than a baby dog! Keep your stuff picked up!

Outdoors

Temptations and dangers also abound in the yard. Check for poisonous plants, bushes with sharp, broken branches at puppy eye level, and trees with dead branches or heavy fruits in danger of falling. Make sure your Chihuahua cannot fall into your pool; for added security, you should teach your Chihuahua to swim and teach her where the steps are. If the steps are still over her head, install a ramp so she can get out of the pool if she ever falls in.

If you take your Chihuahua for a walk, keep her on lead. Too many dangers await a little dog in the big outdoors. She could fall in a storm drain, ditch, or old well, into deep water, or off a high ledge; she could find poisoned animal bait, be caught in wild animal traps, or be caught by a wild animal; she could be attacked by a big dog or hit by a car. Here's a tip: Use a harness in case you must quickly pull your dog to safety in your arms.

Poopy-proofing

The first challenge for new puppy people is to convince their puppy that puppy waste belongs outside. Most people have unrealistic expectations of their dog's ability to become housetrained, based in part upon friends' boasting about their little genius that was housetrained at two weeks of age or something similarly ludicrous. No matter how wonderful and smart your Chihuahua is, she probably will not have full control over her elimination until she is around five months of age, and may not be reliably housetrained until much later.

The best time to start teaching a puppy where to eliminate is between 7 and 9 weeks of age. Before that time, puppies do not seem to learn the concept or to control themselves sufficiently. After 9 weeks of age, they seem to prefer using whatever surface or place they were using between 7 and 9 weeks of age. So it is very important that you make sure your pup has as few chances to go in the wrong places, and as many chances as possible to go in the right places, during this crucial time. This is one reason that dogs raised in indoor X-pens or kennels may be more difficult to housetrain. If they've been raised indoors until after 9 weeks of age, they may not recognize grass or the great outdoors as a bathroom area, and they are slow to accept it as such. You can increase your pup's learning rate by avoiding the following common blunders:

Housetraining blunder #1: Most puppy owners expect too much from their puppies, so they allow their little darlings to wander unsupervised around the house.

Here's the secret: young puppies avoid eliminating in their sleeping and eating area, so if you restrict your puppy to a small area she's less likely to eliminate there and will make an effort to hold herself until you let her out. You can use the crate as her small area, making sure it's not so large that she can simply use one half of it for her bathroom. If your crate is too large, block off part of it with a box or divider.

Confine your puppy when you can't supervise her, but let her out regularly, because if you force her to have accidents in her crate, she'll give up trying to hold it at all. When you let her out, take her immediately to her elimination area. Once she's relieved herself, socialize, play, snuggle, and do all the fun things that makes having a puppy worth all the work.

Once she's housetrained using the crate, expand her den area by placing her bed or crate in a tiny enclosed area—an area only a few feet beyond the boundary of her bed. Do everything you can to prevent her from soiling this area; that is, keep her on a frequent outdoor bathroom break schedule. Gradually expand her area as she goes without soiling it, until eventually she has access to an entire room, and then another room.

If you can't be home to take her out as often as she needs to go, use puppy urine pads (ask for puppy pee pads in the pet store) or sod sections as an indoor potty area. These can be moved outdoors once soiled to teach your puppy to go there. Newspapers are alright in a pinch, but they aren't absorbent.

Housetraining blunder #2: Too many people allow accidents to happen. Puppies have weak control over their bowels, so if you don't give them a chance to go in the right place, they'll have to go in the wrong place. You can't just stick them in a crate or let them roam the house all day and think you won't return home to a messy crate or house and a messier pup. If you cannot be with your puppy for an extended period, you may wish to train her to use a doggy litter box. Several companies now make dog litter that is similar to cat litter but more attractive to dogs. Many Chihuahua owners find a dog litter box is especially handy for rainy days.

Learn to predict when your puppy will have to relieve herself. Immediately after awakening, and soon after heavy drinking or playing, your puppy will urinate. You will probably have to carry a younger baby outside or to her box to get her to the toilet area on time. Right after eating, or if nervous, your puppy will have to defecate. Circling, whining, sniffing, and

generally acting worried usually signals that defecation is imminent. A rule of thumb is that a puppy can, at most, hold its bowels for as many hours as the pup is months old. This means that a three-month-old can hold herself for three hours. If the pup is forced to stay in a crate longer than she can hold herself, you are setting the stage for a big problem.

The more a pup soils in a particular spot, the more likely she is to do it again, partly because the spot smells like urine or feces. This is why it is so critical to never let the pup have an accident indoors; if she does, clean and deodorize the spot thoroughly and block the pup's access to that area. Use a pet deodorizer cleaner, and never use one containing ammonia. Ammonia is a component of urine, so using an ammonia cleaner is like posting a sign that says *"Go here!"*

Housetraining blunder #3: The number three housetraining mistake made by dog owners is overuse of punishment. If the puppy starts to relieve herself inside, quickly but calmly scoop her up and carry her outside (the surprise of being picked up will usually cause her to stop in midstream). You can also clap your hands or make a loud noise to startle her so she stops. You can add a firm *"No,"* but yelling and swatting are actually detrimental. Even if you catch your dog in the act, overly enthusiastic correction tends to teach the dog only not to relieve herself in your presence, even when outside. Punishment doesn't make clear what is desired behavior, but reward makes it clear very quickly. This is why you should reward with a tidbit when the pup does relieve herself outside.

Punishing a dog for a mess made earlier is totally fruitless; it succeeds only in convincing the dog that every once in a while, for no apparent reason, you are apt to go insane and

attack her. It is a perfect recipe for ruining a trusting relationship. That "guilty" look you may think your dog is exhibiting is really fear that you have once again lost your mind.

Housetraining blunder #4: The number four housetraining mistake owners make is to open the door and push the pup outside by herself. After five minutes, the pup is let back in and promptly relieves herself on the rug. Bad dog? No, bad owner. Chances are she spent her time outside huddled by the door trying to get back inside to you. Puppies don't like to be alone, and knowing you are on the other side of the door makes the outdoors unappealing. The solution? You must go outside with her. Don't take her for a walk, don't play with her, simply go with her to her elimination area, say *"Hurry up,"* and be ready to heap on the praise and hand out a treat when she does her deed. Then you can go back inside or stay outside and play.

Now that you've exhausted yourself cleaning and exhausted your checkbook buying, it's time to reap your rewards. Take a break and have some fun with your new Chihuahua chum!

Your Chihuahua expects to be a real member of the family, sharing family activities and supervising the family home. But family members—even Chihuahua family members—need to know the house rules.

Chihuahua Training the Right Way

You don't have to go to obedience classes to train your Chihuahua, although a good class is certainly helpful. But many classes are geared toward handling big, boisterous, out-of-control dogs, and may emphasize force methods and lots of repetition in an attempt to dominate and calm these dogs. Such methods are not good for Chihuahuas—they're not good for any dogs—and if you can't find an instructor who understands that, you're better off training on your own or with some other small-dog owners.

Good dog-training methods have finally caught up with the techniques successful animal trainers have known for years. Old-fashioned force-training methods are ineffective and no fun for either dog or trainer. Chihuahuas are very amenable to training, as long as you use only the gentlest of techniques and keep the following guidelines in mind:

✔ **Guide, don't force.** Chihuahuas already want to please you; your job is to show them how. Forcing them can distract or intimidate them, or even bring that notorious Chi stubborn streak to the surface.

✔ **Punishment doesn't work.** Chihuahuas seldom require anything but the mildest of corrections. Physical corrections can injure small dogs. Striking, shaking, choking, and hanging are extremely dangerous, counterproductive, and cruel; they have no place in the training of a beloved family member. They are the signature of a dumb trainer.

✔ **Accentuate the positive.** Reward your dog for correct behavior; how else can she understand what you want?

✔ **Think like a dog.** Dogs live in the present; if you punish or reward them they can only assume it is for their behavior at that time. So if you discover a mess and drag your dog to it from her nap in the other room and then scold her, the impression to the dog will be that either she is being scolded for napping, or that you're mentally unstable. Dogs cannot understand human language, except for those words you teach them, so you cannot explain to them that their actions of five minutes earlier were bad. Timing is everything in a correction. If you discover your dog in the midst of mischief, say *"No!"* emphatically while she's still doing what you don't want her to do, not after you've snatched her up and put her outside.

✔ **You get what you ask for.** Dogs repeat actions that bring them rewards whether you intend them to or not. Letting your Chihuahua out of her crate to make her quit whining might work momentarily, but in the long run you will end up with a dog that whines incessantly every time you put her in a crate. Make sure you reward only those behaviors you want to see more often.

✔ **Mean what you say.** Sometimes a puppy can be awfully cute when she misbehaves, sometimes your hands are full, and sometimes you just aren't sure what you want from your dog. But lapses in consistency are ultimately unfair to the dog. Intermittent payoffs produce behavior that is most resistant to change. If you feed your dog from the table because she begs "just this one time," you teach her that while begging may not always result in a handout, you

never know—it just might pay off tonight. You could hardly do a better job of training your Chi to beg if you tried.

✔ **Say what you mean.** Your Chihuahua takes commands literally. If you teach her that *"Down"* means to lie down, then what must she think when you command *"Down"* to tell her to get off the sofa where she was already lying down? Or *"Sit down"* when you mean *"Sit?"* If *"Stay"* means not to move until you say she can, and you say *"Stay here"* as you leave the house for work, do you really want her to sit by the door all day until you get home?

✔ **Will work for food.** Your Chihuahua will work better for training sessions if her stomach is not full, and she will be more responsive to food rewards.

✔ **Happy endings.** Keep sessions short and fun, no longer than 10 to 15 minutes. Begin and end each training session with something your dog can do well.

✔ **Your Chihuahua didn't read the book.** Nothing will ever go just as perfectly as it seems to in all the training instructions. Just remember to be consistent, firm, gentle, realistic, and patient, and most of all, keep your sense of humor.

Tools of the Trade

Just as training methods have changed, so has equipment. Gone are the choke collars of the jerk-and-pull school. Positive training methods favor a buckle or martingale collar, which tightens enough to prevent escape but not as much as a traditional choke collar. A 6-foot (1.8-m) lightweight leash, and a 10-foot (3.1-m) light-line complete the

Chihuahua's leash wardrobe. You can also add a hollow tube such as PVC pipe to run your leash through so you can guide your ground-level dog in directions other than straight up.

Training clickers are available from most pet supply catalogs; you can substitute anything small that makes a quick, unusual sound (see page 32). Your training outfit will need pockets or a treat pouch, and you'll need lots and lots of little treats to put in them. Bits of cat food, semimoist food, cheese, or dried liver are ideal.

By far the most essential piece of Chihuahua training equipment, though, is a bottomless supply of patience and enthusiasm.

Quick Studies

Just because your Chihuahua lives a life of leisure doesn't mean she can't learn a new trick or two. For years Chihuahuas were never given enough credit for their intelligence; people equated their small bodies with small minds—at least, people who didn't know them. Chihuahua people have always known that Chis pack more IQ per pound than any other dog, but because Chihuahuas didn't hunt or herd or guard they didn't have the opportunity to show off like some other breeds. Now obedience and agility trials are giving them a chance to show what they can do. But you don't have to set your sights on competition to enjoy training your

Chihuahua. You'll find that training is fun for both of you; besides, even a Chihuahua has to have some schooling!

The Click Is the Trick

Clicker training is based on professional animal training techniques and is fast becoming popular with dog trainers. In clicker training you teach the dog that a "click" sound signals a coming reward. Clickers are sold at most large pet supply stores. A clicker signal is used because it is fast, noticeable, and something the dog otherwise does not encounter in everyday life. Once the dog associates the click with an upcoming reward, you then wait for the dog to do the behavior you want her to do. The instant she does so, you click to tell the dog her behavior is going to pay off. Then you give her a treat. If the dog makes a mistake, nothing happens. You just wait for her to do it right, giving her guidance when possible. In essence, the dog thinks she is training you because she realizes whenever she does a certain behavior she makes you click, and then reward, her.

Now let's use the clicker to train our Chihuahua, Isis, to sit.

✔ First we put her up on something such as a chair or bed or table so we can reach her and she doesn't run off. Then we click and then reward her several times so she realizes a click means a treat is coming her way. Give tiny treats; it may take 100 click-treat pairings before she makes the connection!

✔ When she's associating the click with a treat we introduce the command, in this case, *"Sit."* For any command in which we want her to do something, we start by saying her name: *"Isis, sit."*

✔ We wait a millisecond after the command before we help her perform what is wanted. That's because the crux of training lies in anticipation; she will come to anticipate that behavior following the command. We also want to get her to do the behavior without being forced to do it.

✔ Immediately after saying *"Isis, sit"* we lure her front end up by holding a treat above and just behind her muzzle. If she jumps up for it, we don't give it to her. If she bends her hind legs to get to the treat, we click, then reward. We do it again, clicking and rewarding for

successively closer approximations to the *sit* position.

✔ Finally, she sits, we click, we treat; Isis is happy, we're happy. Isis thinks she's the one training us, we think we're the ones training her—but does it really matter as long as she sits?

We can use the same concept to teach Isis to lie down, come, heel, speak, roll over, or do anything she naturally does on her own. But remember, it takes time and you must work for small increments of improvement. To teach the *stay*, we begin with only a few seconds, and step only a few feet away from her, saying after, *"Isis, stay!";* then we click and reward. We repeat until she's reliable at that time and distance before pushing our luck. We want to reward success, not punish failure. For example, to teach Isis to heel, instead of dragging her back to *heel* position, we ignore her until she happens to be in *heel* position for a second. Instantly we click and treat; then we gradually require her to stay there longer, and add some zigzags and turns, until she discovers being in *heel* position turns us into human snack machines.

Chihuahua Chat

Despite being dubbed "man's best friend," the relationship between human and dog is a one-sided one. People expect their dogs to understand them, seldom bothering to try to learn the dog's language. With very little effort, you can meet your Chihuahua halfway, and learn to speak Chihuahuan.

As much as they have shaken off their wild vestiges, Chihuahuas still speak the ancestral language of wolves:

✔ A wagging tail and lowered head upon greeting signals submission.

✔ A lowered body, tucked rear, urination, and perhaps even rolling over signals extreme submission.

✔ A yawn may signal nervousness. Drooling and panting can signal extreme nervousness (or car sickness!).

✔ Exposed teeth, raised hackles, upright posture, stiff-legged gait, and direct stare signal very dominant behavior.

✔ Elbows on the ground, rear in the air, and a wagging tail signal an invitation to play!

Behavior Problems

Even the best dogs with the best owners can sometimes do the worst things. Too often distraught owners get their training advice from the next-door neighbor or dog trainers who don't have a scientific background in dog behavior. Veterinarians can sometimes offer advice, but few are extensively trained in behavior. Fortunately, great strides have been made in recent years in canine behavioral therapy. Before despairing, consult a certified canine behaviorist, who may employ a combination of conditioning and drug therapy to achieve a cure. As a first step in any serious behavior problem, a thorough veterinary exam should be performed.

House Soiling

If your previously house-trained adult Chihuahua begins to urinate or defecate in the house, it could indicate a physical or emotional problem. A physical examination is warranted any time a formerly house-trained dog begins to soil the house. You and your veterinarian will need to consider the following possibilities:

✔ Older dogs may simply not have the bladder control they had as youngsters; a doggy door or doggy litter box, plus a veterinary exam, are indicated.

✔ Older spayed females may "dribble." Ask your veterinarian about drug therapies.

✔ Frequent urination of small amounts, especially if the urine is bloody or dark, may indicate a bladder infection. A veterinary exam is indicated.

✔ Sometimes a house-trained dog will be forced to soil the house because of a bout of diarrhea, and afterward will continue to soil in the same area. If this happens, restrict the dog from that area, deodorize the area with an enzymatic cleaner, and revert to basic housetraining lessons.

✔ Male dogs may "lift their leg" inside of the house as a means of marking it as theirs. Castration may solve this problem; otherwise, diligent deodorizing and the use of some dog-deterring odorants (available at pet stores) may help. Also try reverting to basic housetraining. "Belly bands," which are bands of absorbent material fastened with Velcro around an incorrigible leg lifter's abdomen, are often helpful.

✔ Submissive dogs, especially young females, may urinate upon greeting you; punishment only makes this submissive urination worse. For these dogs, be careful not to bend over them or otherwise dominate them and to keep greetings calm. Submissive urination is usually outgrown as the dog gains more confidence.

✔ Some dogs defecate or urinate from the stress of separation anxiety; you must treat the anxiety to cure the symptom. Dogs that mess their crate when left in it are usually suffering from separation anxiety or anxiety about being closed in a crate. Other telltale signs of anxiety-produced elimination are drooling, scratching, and escape-oriented behavior. You need to treat separation anxiety (see the discussion under Home Destruction, below) and start crate training over, placing the pup in it for a short period of time and working up gradually to longer times. Dogs that suffer from crate anxiety but not separation anxiety do better if left loose in a dog-proofed room.

Home Destruction

One of the most common, and commonly misunderstood, dog behavior problems is home destruction. Even a tiny Chihuahua can do considerable damage when properly motivated. Owners too often assume their dog is spiting them for being left. They're wrong. Owners who continue to believe this erroneous idea never cure their dogs. Remember: *Dogs never destroy out of spite.*

Separation anxiety: Being left alone is stressful for highly social animals, including dogs. Chihuahuas and their people tend to bond closely, and Chihuahuas often become so dependent on their people that they are highly stressed when those people are gone. They react by becoming agitated and trying to escape from confinement. Perhaps they reason that if they can just get out of the house they will be reunited with their people. The telltale signature of a dog suffering from separation anxiety is focus of destruction around doors and windows. Most people punish the dog for this behavior. Unfortunately, punishment is ineffective because it increases the anxiety

level of the dog, as she comes to both look forward to and dread her owner's return.

The proper therapy is treatment of the dog's fear of being left alone. This is done by leaving her alone for very short periods of time, gradually working up to longer periods. Take care that the dog is never left long enough to become anxious during any session. When you return home, refrain from a joyous reunion scene—and try not to scream in despair either. No matter what the condition of the home, greet the dog calmly or even ignore her for a few minutes, to emphasize the point that being left was really no big deal. Then have her perform a simple trick or obedience exercise so that you have an excuse to praise her. It takes a lot of patience, and often a whole lot of self-control, but it's not fair to you or your dog to let this situation continue.

Entertainment: Not all home destruction arises from separation anxiety. Puppies are natural demolition dogs. The best cure (besides adulthood) is supervision. Adult Chihuahuas still may destroy items through frustration or boredom. The best way to deal with these dogs is to provide both physical interaction, such as chasing a ball, and mental interaction, such as practicing a few tricks, an hour or so before leaving. Have a supply of toys handy that you give your dog only when you're gone.

Rotate which toys you hand out so your dog doesn't get bored with them. Several interactive toys are available that can provide hours of entertainment; for example, some can be filled with treats such as peanut butter, in such a way that it takes the dog a very long time to extract the treat from the toy.

Fearfulness

Even the bravest of Chihuahuas can develop irrational fears. The cardinal rule of working with a fearful dog is to never push the dog into situations that might be overwhelming. A program of gradual desensitization, with the dog exposed to the frightening person or thing and then rewarded for calm behavior, is time-consuming but the best way to alleviate any fear.

Never coddle your Chihuahua when she acts afraid, because it reinforces the behavior. It is always useful if your dog knows a few simple commands; performing these exercises correctly gives you a reason to praise her and also increases the dog's sense of security because she knows what is expected of her. Whether it is a fear of strangers, dogs, car rides, thunder, or being left alone, the concept is the same: Never hurry, and never push the dog to the point that she is afraid.

Strangers: Many Chihuahuas can be cautious about strangers. Never force a dog that is afraid of people to be petted by somebody she doesn't know; it won't help her overcome her fear and it's a good way for the stranger to get nipped. Strangers should be asked to ignore shy dogs, even when approached by the dog. Dogs fear the attention of a stranger more than they fear the strangers themselves; often the shy dog will quietly come to investi-

gate the new person if the person pays attention to something else. When the dog gets braver, have the stranger offer a treat, at first while not even looking at the dog. Caution strangers not to stare at your dog—staring a dog directly in the eye is interpreted by the dog as a threat. It can cause a fearful dog to bite or run.

Thunder: Fear of thunder is a common problem in older dogs. Try to avoid it by acting cheerful, playing with your dog, and rewarding her with treats for calm behavior when a thunderstorm strikes. Once a dog develops a thunder phobia, try to find a recording of a thunderstorm. Some mobile apps, for example, have storm sounds, but you will need to play them louder eventually. Play it at a very low level and reward your dog for calm behavior. Gradually increase the intensity and duration of the recording.

That doesn't mean you should tolerate fear-based aggression. Work with your dog to get her over her fears (see the section about fearful behavior, page 37). If she remains unpredictable, don't place her in situations that could arouse her fear or cause her to bite. Even if she doesn't do a lot of damage, a biting dog of any size is frightening to most people and she could cause an accident or be hurt herself.

Jumping Up

Puppies naturally greet their mother and other adult dogs by licking them around the corners of their mouth. This behavior

Aggression

In some breeds aggression often results from a dog's attempts to dominate its owners. This is virtually never the case in Chihuahuas. True, some Chihuahuas can be little dictators, but most of them are simply one-person dogs that are either protective of their special person or of their own safety.

Chihuahuas are at the mercy of the people around them. Consider how they must feel when you pick them up and hand them to a stranger. If you do this, hand them rear end first, which seems to be less intimidating for them, and less likely to cause them to snap.

Some dogs are afraid of children, either because they don't understand what they are or because they've had bad experiences with them. Rambunctious children can be frightening to a tiny dog. Introduce dogs and children carefully, encouraging the child to offer the dog a treat and stroke her gently.

translates to humans, but in order to reach your face they need to jump up on you. Of course, Chihuahuas would need to pole-vault to reach your face, but they still try, instead succeeding only in scratching your knees to shreds. Most owners can't resist the temptation to bend down and pick up the little jumping bean so they can share a face-to-face greeting. That's fine, but it does teach the dog that she will be rewarded if she jumps on you. It's better to teach your Chihuahua a special command that lets her know when you want to pick her up; otherwise, don't reward her for jumping up.

Barking

Having a doggy doorbell can be handy, but there is a difference between a dog that warns you of a suspicious stranger and one that warns you of oxygen in the air. The surest way to make your neighbors dislike your dog is to let her bark unchecked. Allow your Chihuahua to bark momentarily at strangers, and then call her to you and praise her for quiet behavior, distracting her with an obedience exercise if need be.

Isolated dogs will often bark from frustration or as a means of getting attention and alleviating loneliness. Even if the attention gained includes punishment, the dog will continue to bark in order to obtain the temporary presence of a person. The simplest solution is to move the dog's quarters to a less isolated location. For example, if barking occurs when your pup is put to bed, move her bed into your bedroom. Do this before she goes to bed and starts barking, so she doesn't think she's being rewarded for raising a ruckus. If this isn't possible, the

pup's quiet behavior must be rewarded by your presence, working up to gradually longer and longer periods. The distraction of a special chew toy, given only at bedtime, may help alleviate barking. The pup that must spend the day home alone is a greater challenge. Again, the simplest solution is to change the situation, perhaps by adding another animal—a good excuse to get two Chihuahuas?

Remember, the only perfectly behaved dog is a stuffed one, but they're not nearly as much fun and as loving as a Chihuahua, even if the living version does occasionally get into trouble.

CHIHUAHUA CHALLENGES

She's mastered lap sitting. She excels at copiloting. Sometimes she even comes when she's called. Yet that's not enough for some people, and for some Chihuahuas; instead, they look for more challenges. And they can find plenty of them in the world of canine competitions.

The dog world has contests for smart dogs, pretty dogs, agile dogs, trailing dogs, and even dancing dogs. Some are easy enough that most dogs can succeed with a little effort on your part; some are so fiendishly difficult they can make you question your sanity for trying. But they're all fun.

The Chihuahua Good Citizen

One of the most important challenges is the AKC Canine Good Citizen test, which was developed to formally recognize dogs that behave in public. Its requirements include abilities that any well-mannered dog should possess, such as:

✔ Allowing a friendly stranger to greet you, without showing shyness or aggression, and without approaching the stranger.

✔ Sitting politely for petting by a stranger.

✔ Allowing a stranger to examine her ears, feet, and body, and to lightly groom her, without showing shyness or resentment; she should also be clean and healthy appearing.

✔ Walking politely on a loose leash alongside you through several turns, stopping when you stop.

✔ Walking on a leash through a group of people, without pulling, shying from, or jumping up on them.

✔ Sitting and lying down on command and staying in place while on a 20-foot (6.1-m) line while you are 20 feet away.

✔ Staying and then coming when called from 10 feet (3.1-m) away.

✔ Behaving politely to another dog that approaches with his handler.

✔ Reacting calmly to distractions such as dropped chairs or passing joggers.

✔ Remaining calmly for three minutes in your absence, while being held on a leash by a stranger.

Your dog doesn't have to be AKC-registered to receive a certificate. Unlike formal obedience, precision isn't necessary and you can talk

═══ TIP ═══

Careful!

Dog competitions are crowded and hectic events, and dog owners there are often distracted and put too much trust in their dogs. It takes only a moment for a big dog that has never seen a tiny dog to mistake it for a mutant squirrel and go after it. Don't take chances at such events. Hold your dog or keep her in a carrier when around other dogs you don't know.

and encouragement from people who are experienced obedience competitors and fellow dog lovers. They provide an environment filled with distractions similar to those you would encounter at actual trial.

Obedience is teamwork; it's not a demonstration of how you can dominate your dog. Both of you should be acting as a team and enjoying the exercises; if you're not, add some games and try to come up with ways to make sure your Chihuahua is having as much fun as you are. If you enter obedience competition with your Chihuahua, remember this as your Golden Rule: Companion Dogs need Companion Persons; a person who gets upset because of a failed trial is missing the point. Failing a trial, in the scope of life, is an insignificant event. Never let a title or a ribbon become more important than a trusting relationship with your companion. Besides, your Chihuahua will forgive you for the times you mess up!

to your dog throughout. Urinating or defecating during an exercise, or behaving aggressively to a dog or person, will cause your dog to fail, though; after all, these would not normally be considered proper public behaviors!

Brain Power

How smart is your Chihuahua? You may find that your Chihuahua is a canine Einstein that enjoys learning new skills. You plan on training your Chihuahua the commands *heel, sit, down, come,* and *stay* for use in everyday life. Add *stand,* and your dog will have the basic skills necessary to earn entry level AKC Rally or Obedience titles. Higher degrees require retrieving, jumping, hand signals, and scent discrimination.

Obedience clubs offer advanced classes that involve jumping, retrieving, hand signals, and all sorts of challenging exercises. They can also guide you toward earning an obedience title. Classes are valuable sources of training advice

Mexican Jumping Beings

The sport of agility combines athletic and mental abilities as dogs jump, sprint, climb, balance, and weave on an obstacle course of tunnels, seesaws, balance beams, jumps, and weave poles. It's the most fun your dog can have without breaking any rules! Many obedience clubs are now sponsoring agility training, but you can start some of the fundamentals at home. Entice your dog to walk through a tunnel made of sheets draped over chairs or through a child's play tunnel; guide her with treats to weave in and out of a series of poles made from several plumber's helpers placed in line; make her comfortable walking on a wide raised board; teach her to jump through

a tire and over a small hurdle. If you can't find a club to train with, you can make your own equipment. Contact the AKC, USDAA, or UKC for regulations (see Information, page 93, for addresses).

Show-offs

If you have gone out of your way to get a show-quality Chihuahua, chances are you will want to show her. Conformation shows evaluate your Chihuahua on the basis of the official breed standard (see page 90). A judge will examine each dog from nose to tail, feeling her body structure, studying her way of moving, and looking at the total picture she creates.

Chihuahuas are easy to show, but even the best dog needs a little work before showing off. Practice posing your Chihuahua on a table with all four feet pointing forward, legs parallel to each other and perpendicular to the ground, and head and tail held high.

Practice also having your Chihuahua trot in a straight line beside you, again with head and tail held high and proud. The most common mistake new handlers make is to demand that their dogs stand like statues for so long the poor dogs become bored and begin to hate showing.

Foster a happy attitude, which is a great asset for a show dog. Professional handlers can show your dog for you and probably win more often than you would, but it's more fun to do it yourself!

Points

At an AKC show, each time a judge chooses your dog as the best dog of its sex that is not

CHECKLIST

Show Grooming

Grooming for the show ring begins long before the show.

1. Overly thick winter coats need to go. Use a rubber brush to remove dead hair.
2. Dandruff-prone dogs are best washed a few days (rather than immediately) before the show.
3. A mink oil spray rubbed in on the day of the show can help the coat shine.
4. Long coats should be dried so that they aren't too puffy.
5. Many people cut the vibrissae (whiskers) for a neater and more professional appearance, but leaving these important sensory organs intact is becoming more fashionable.

already a Champion, it wins up to 5 points, depending upon how many dogs it defeats. To become an AKC Champion (Ch.) your Chihuahua must win 15 points, including two majors (that is, defeating enough dogs to win 3 to 5 points at a time).

If you are lucky enough to win Best of Breed, be sure to stick around to compete in the toy group later in the day. The winner of the toy group then competes with the winner of the other six groups for the Best in Show award.

To survive as a conformation competitor you must be able to separate your own ego and self-esteem from your dog. You also must not allow your dog's ability to win in the ring cloud your perception of your dog's true worth in her primary role: that of friend and companion.

Your Chihuahua never has to step foot in a show ring, earn a title, or thrill anyone except you to be first place in your heart.

La Chihuahua Cha-cha-cha

Okay, admit it. Sometimes when the drapes are drawn and the radio is blasting and it's just you and your dog, you've tried to dance with your Chihuahua. Of course she probably just stood there with a stunned look on her face, but do you blame her? You probably were not dancing up to her expectations. But eventually she forgave you and caught on to the fun. Now you can actually do the Chihuahua Cucaracha in public—even in competition—in a sport known as canine freestyle. Six-footed dance teams boogie, waltz, and do-si-do to music, sometimes even in costume. Just be careful you decide who gets to lead, and if you choose to flamenco, watch your step! Who says a good dance partner can't have two left feet?

Doctor Chihuahua

While it's fun to compete for trophies and titles, far more rewarding challenges can be found closer to home. Chihuahuas excel at many roles, but perhaps one of the most important is that of canine therapist. Studies have shown that pet ownership increases life

expectancy and that petting animals can lower blood pressure. In recent years nursing home residents and hospitalized children have come to look forward to visits by dogs, including Chihuahuas. These dogs must be meticulously well mannered and well groomed. To be registered as a Certified Therapy Dog a dog must demonstrate that he will act in an obedient, outgoing, gentle manner to strangers. Don't forget your own shut-in neighbors who may welcome a daily visit from you and your dog. Chihuahuas may be small, but their big hearts can make a huge difference in somebody's life.

Getting There

Traveling to events is half the fun of getting involved in them. A canine copilot has good and bad points. A dog gives you a good excuse to see out-of-the-way nature sights, but she also restricts you from a lot of activities. You can't leave your dog in the car while you shop if the weather is hot, as it's too easy for your dog to die of heatstroke. Nor can you leave the windows open because your dog could jump out or someone could reach in and take her. The best solution is to travel with your dog in a crate that is in turn fastened securely and even padlocked to your car. Not only does this let you leave your dog for a very short while with the windows down, but it also acts as a safety belt when you're moving, saving your dog from hurtling into the dashboard when you slam on the brakes.

If you stay in a motel, consider yourself lucky you've found one that still allows dogs. So many people think their dogs are above the rules that they've allowed them to christen

Walking and Jogging

Sometimes the best activities are those in your own neighborhood.

✔ Take your dog for a walk, or form a dog walking group. Walking is excellent exercise for both people and dogs. Keep up a brisk pace, and gradually work up to longer distances.

✔ For a walk around the neighborhood, use a harness or a martingale collar that cannot slip over your Chihuahua's head. Retractable leashes are great for walks, but you must be especially vigilant when using them because dogs can still dart out into the path of traffic when on them.

✔ Pick your dog up or keep her close around strange dogs.

✔ Check the footpads regularly for abrasions, gravel, or blistering from hot pavement.

✔ In winter, check between the pads for balls of ice and rinse the feet when returning from walking on rock salt.

✔ Be careful in hot weather. Dogs can't cool themselves as well as humans can, and heatstroke has taken the lives of far too many dogs on warm days.

the rugs, gnaw on the furniture, and bark unchecked to the point that motel owners feel they can't afford to let dogs check in. If you've found a motel willing to take a chance, don't let it, and other dog owners, down. Otherwise, you may be sleeping in your car next time.

It's great fun to enter competitions with your Chihuahua, and even more fun to win at them. But the wonderful thing about Chihuahuas is that they are as agile racing around the living room's obstacles as they are racing around an agility ring's obstacles; they look as beautiful scanning the yard for squirrels as they do posing in the show ring; and they are as wonderful companion dogs snoozing in your lap as they are winning High in Trial. Besides, what better prize is there than your Chihuahua's heart?

KEEPING UP APPEARANCES

Does your dirty-looking Chihuahua give you dirty looks? Chihuahuas feel their best when they look their best. They look their best when their coat, skin, teeth, eyes, and ears are groomed and clean. Done regularly, both of you can come to look forward to grooming as a special bonding time.

Skin and Coat Care

Grooming a Chihuahua isn't difficult—it's not as if you have a huge area to cover! Nor do you need extravagant grooming equipment to get the job done. Just make it a daily date to share a few minutes of grooming.

Coats: For short coats, use a natural bristle brush to distribute oils, a rubber bristle brush to remove dead hair, and a flea comb to check for fleas. For long coats, use a pin brush or wide-tooth comb. If you come across a mat—most often behind the ears—spray some hair de-tangler in it and then gently pull the mat apart along its long axis with your fingers. Pull the hair out of the mat, rather than the mat out of the hair.

Shedding: Dogs kept indoors under artificial lighting shed year-round, with a major shedding season in the spring. A daily vigorous brushing using a bristle or rubber curry brush is the best way to hurry along shedding. More hair will shed after bathing, and dead hairs are especially easy to dislodge when the coat is still damp. A rubber shedding mitt or large rubber bristle brush may help pull out undercoat, especially from thicker coats.

Feet: If your dog has long hair on her feet, you can trim that to prevent slipping or tracking in mud. Errant hairs elsewhere can be snipped off, but there's really little to trim on most dogs. Even in the show ring, very little trimming is desired.

Home Remedies

Coat disasters can be treated with a number of home remedies.

✔ Remove tar by coating it with vegetable oil and then washing it with detergent.

✔ Remove pine tar by soaking it with hairspray.

✔ Brighten and fluff a drab dirty coat by brushing in cornstarch.

✔ Remove eye and lip stains on light coats by carefully applying a mixture of hydrogen peroxide, cornstarch, and milk of magnesia, and then just as carefully brushing it off with a soft toothbrush.

✔ Remove spots of dirt when there's no time for a bath by using a rinse-free dog shampoo that is applied to the coat and then simply rubbed dry.

Bathing

Your Chihuahua will be more pleasant to pet and hold if she gets a bath. Bathe her in a sink, preferably one with a spray attachment. Place a towel in the bottom so she won't slip, and make sure you have a way to hold your slippery Chihuahua if she decides she's had enough and tries to jump out when your hands are full. Use warm water and wet her down starting at her rear and working toward her head.

Shampoo: Use a shampoo made for dogs. Dog skin has a pH of 7.5, whereas human skin has a pH of 5.5; bathing in a shampoo formulated for human pH won't give optimal results, and in some cases can cause flaking. You don't need flea shampoo; most shampoos will kill fleas anyway, and if your dog has a flea problem you're better off getting a flea product from your veterinarian. Dogs with skin problems can profit from a variety of therapeutic shampoos. Dry scaly skin is treated with moisturizing shampoos, excessive flaking or oiliness is treated with antiseborrheic shampoo, itchy skin with oatmeal-based shampoo, and damaged skin with antimicrobial shampoo.

Take care that shampoo doesn't get in your dog's eyes, and that water doesn't get in her ears. After working in the shampoo, rinse it out thoroughly beginning at the head and working backward. You can follow with a crème rinse, which will make the coat softer and, in the case of long hairs, lie closer.

Blow drying: Don't let your dog outside on a chilly day when still damp from a bath. You have removed the oils from the coat and saturated her down to the skin, removing the coat's insulating ability. A blow dryer is the best way to dry your Chihuahua on a chilly day, but it needs to be introduced gradually. Never leave a Chihuahua in a crate with a blow dryer aimed at her; many dogs have died from overheating this way.

Chihuahuas have generally healthy skin. Sometimes those with blue (gray) coats have thinner hair and more sensitive skin, but any dog can have some of the following common skin problems.

✔ **Dandruff:** Dandruff can have several causes. It occurs more often in winter when indoor heating dries the skin. Keep your dog well hydrated by offering tasty liquids to drink. Wash her with a shampoo containing salicylic acid or sulfur. Follow the bath with a crème rinse to seal in moisture. Use one with colloidal oatmeal if her skin is dry and itchy. To remove dandruff use a flea comb or wipe the coat with a nylon stocking.

✔ **Bad odor:** Bad odor can come not only from skin problems, but also mouth, ear, anal, or genital problems. Smelly saliva from bad teeth can make her fur stink when she licks herself. Impacted anal sacs can also contribute to bad odor. Don't ignore bad odor, and don't make your dog take the blame for something you need to fix. She doesn't want to smell bad, either!

✔ **Skin allergies:** Itchy skin often points to allergies. Inhalant allergies usually cause itchy skin, typically first appearing in young dogs and worsening with age. Even allergies to food tend to express themselves by causing itchy skin. The main sites of itching are the face, ears, feet, forelegs, armpits, and abdomen. With flea allergies, the rump, legs, and paws are mainly affected.

Allergens can be isolated with an intradermal skin test, in which small amounts of various allergen extracts are injected under the skin. The skin is then monitored for localized allergic reactions.

✔ **External parasites:** Look for fleas or their telltale flea dirt (black specks that look like pepper but turn reddish when they get wet) around the neck, chest, belly, rump, and anal area. The best way to check is with a flea comb, but you can also part the hair and just look.

Ticks can be found anywhere on the dog, but most often burrow around the ears, neck, chest, and between the toes. To remove a tick, use a tissue or tweezers, since some diseases can be transmitted to humans. Grasp the tick as close to the skin as possible, and pull slowly and steadily, trying not to leave the head in the dog. Don't squeeze the tick, as this can inject its contents into the dog. Clean the site with alcohol. Often a bump will remain after the tick is removed, even if you got it all out. The bump will go away with time.

It used to be a challenge to keep a dog flea-free. Now with new products there is no excuse for any dog, much less a little Chihuahua, to be crawling with fleas, mites, and ticks. Forget the old flea sprays. New flea control products really do work. Vary the type you use, if possible, so that your flea population doesn't select fleas immune to one particular type.

Some of these products are also effective on ticks and even mange and ear mites. Remember, external parasites not only make your dog miserable with itching, but can transmit internal parasites and systemic diseases. For example, fleas transmit tapeworms, and ticks transmit several diseases including ehrlichiosis and Rocky Mountain spotted fever.

Ear Care

Chihuahuas tend to have healthy ears because their pricked ears allow air to circulate down into the canal. The canal otherwise tends to remain moist and warm, a perfect hothouse in which all sorts of unwanted things can incubate. Remember that unlike the human ear, the canine ear canal is made up of an initial long vertical segment that then abruptly angles to run horizontally toward the skull. Most outer ear infections are hidden from view in this horizontal section. Keeping your Chihuahua's ears clean and dry will help them stay healthy. Even so, ear problems can crop up.

Signs of ear problems: Signs of ear problems include inflammation, discharge, debris, foul odor, pain, scratching, shaking, tilting of the head, or circling to one side. Bacterial and yeast infections, ear mites or ticks, foreign bodies, inhalant allergies, seborrhea, or hypothyroidism are possible underlying problems. Because the ear canal is lined with skin, any skin disorder that affects the dog elsewhere can also strike its ears.

Treatment: If your dog has dirty ears, but doesn't appear to have any discomfort, you can try cleaning the ear yourself with an ear cleaning solution available from your veterinarian. Flood the canal with solution and massage it in so it goes down the horizontal section of the canal. Then let go and jump away—of course you've thought ahead and are doing this outside! If the ear has so much debris that repeated rinses don't clean it right up, you have a problem that will need veterinary attention. If the ear is red, swollen, or painful, do not attempt to clean it yourself. Your dog may need to be sedated for cleaning, and may have a serious problem. Cleaning solutions will flush debris but will not kill mites or cure infections.

Ear Mites

Before rinsing away ear debris, examine it. Debris that looks like dry wax mixed with coffee grounds is one indication of ear mites. Sometimes the tiny mites can even be seen with a magnifying glass if the material is placed on a dark background. A dog with ear

mites will scratch its ears, shake its head, and perhaps hold its head sideways and ears down. Ear mites are highly contagious and intensely irritating. Separate a dog with ear mites from other pets and wash your hands after handling its ears. Your veterinarian can provide the best medication, and may suggest treating any other dogs or cats in your home.

Eye Care

Chihuahuas tend to have healthy eyes, which is a good thing, since they're so big and soulful! But their size, coupled with their position at ground level, can predispose them to corneal abrasions from underbrush or blowing debris. If you think your dog has a scratched cornea,

perhaps because she's squinting or tearing, ask your veterinarian about applying some lubricating ophthalmic ointment. If it doesn't get better in a day, it's time for a veterinary visit.

A thick mucus discharge usually indicates a problem that requires veterinary attention. A clear watery discharge can be a symptom of a foreign body, allergies, or a tear drainage problem. A clogged tear drainage duct can cause the tears to drain onto the face rather than the normal drainage through the nose. Your veterinarian can diagnose a drainage problem with a simple test.

Many Chihuahuas' eyes water excessively for no apparent reason. Wiping the tears away several times daily will minimize tear staining, but won't prevent it. A quick but temporary fix

can be achieved by applying a mixture of equal parts hydrogen peroxide, milk of magnesia, and cornstarch to the stained fur, allowing it to dry, and gently brushing it away.

Other eye problems can cause squinting, redness, itching, tearing, dullness, mucus discharge, or a change in pupil size or reactivity. Anytime your dog's pupils do not react to

light or when one eye reacts differently from another, take her to the veterinarian immediately. It could indicate a serious ocular or neurological problem.

Nail Care

The pampered life of the average Chihuahua is not conducive to wearing down its nails. It doesn't herd sheep for miles, hunt for its dinner, or even dig out vermin, all activities that help keep nails a healthy length. So you have to do *your* part and cut your dog's nails at least once a month. Long nails cause discomfort and may eventually cause splayed feet and even lameness. They can get snagged, pulling the nail from its bed or dislocating the toe. The dewclaws (the rudimentary "thumbs" on the wrists) can get caught on things even more easily and can be ripped out or actually loop around and grow into the dog's leg.

Nail trimming: You can hold your Chihuahua upside down on your lap when you cut her nails. Use a sharp nail trimmer so that it cuts, rather than crushes, the nail. Viewed from beneath the nail, you will see a solid core culminating in a hollowed nail. Cut the tip up to the core, but not beyond. On occasion you will slip up and cause the nail to bleed. Apply styptic powder to the nail to stop the bleeding. If this is not available, dip the nail in flour or hold it to a wet teabag. And be more careful next time! Always end a nail trimming session with a treat.

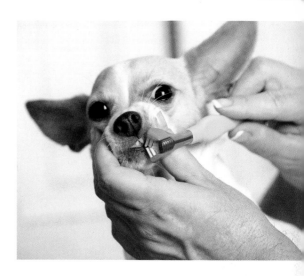

Dental Care

Small dogs tend to have more dental problems than do large dogs, so it's important that you keep your Chihuahua's teeth clean and healthy from the start. The most important dental care you can give your Chihuahua is regular toothbrushing. Meat-flavored dog toothpaste helps your dog enjoy the process. Dry food and hard dog biscuits, carrots, rawhide, and dental chewies are helpful in removing plaque, but can't do the job that brushing does.

If not removed, plaque will attract bacteria and minerals, which will harden into tartar. Plaque can cause infections to form along the gum line, then spread rootward causing irreversible periodontal disease with tissue, bone, and tooth loss. The bacteria may also sometimes enter the bloodstream and cause infection in the kidneys and heart valves.

Long-coat Chihuahuas can sometimes get their own hair tangled around their teeth at the gum line, eventually causing infection. Examine your dog's teeth and gums once a week for redness, swelling, or any signs of discomfort. Pawing at the mouth can indicate a foreign object stuck between the teeth, under or around the tongue, or across the roof of the mouth. Swelling on the muzzle in front of or just below an eye can indicate an infection of one of the large upper teeth in the rear of the mouth, a situation that requires veterinary attention.

Tiny dogs sometimes have problems with dental occlusion that result from the failure of baby teeth to fall out when they are supposed to. Most often the new permanent tooth will come in and the baby tooth will remain alongside it, crowding the permanent tooth from its rightful position. If this condition persists for more than a week, your veterinarian may suggest removing the baby tooth.

Good grooming is one of the foundations of good health and good relationships. You wouldn't feel your best if you had to walk around with dirty teeth and hair. Neither would your dog!

Little dogs can have big appetites. That's good, because they also have big nutritional requirements. How do you supply a diet that packs enough nutrients per pound to fuel up your Chihuahua without fattening him up?

Chihuahua Weight

The problem with feeding little hungry dogs is that they can't eat much food without becoming little fat dogs. They can easily fill up on morsels of junk food and then have little room left for healthy food. A potato chip here, a cookie there, and maybe a few licks of ice cream wouldn't make much difference to the diet of a big dog, but they can make a huge difference to the diet of a little dog. And any self-respecting Chihuahua knows how to get her people to give her anything she wants. No wonder so many Chihuahuas look like engorged ticks on four sticks!

A Chihuahua in proper weight should never look or feel fat. Viewed from either the top or side, your Chi should have a definite waistline. She should not have a dimple at the tail base or a ripple of fat over the shoulders. You should be able to just feel the ribs when you run your hands along the rib cage. Proper Chihuahua weight depends on the bone structure and size of your dog, but in general the so-called pocket-sized or teacup Chihuahuas weigh less than 3 pounds (1.4 kg); a small Chihuahua weighs about 4 pounds (1.8 kg), and the AKC Standard calls for an upper weight limit of 6 pounds (2.7 kg).

Fat Chihuahuas can't run and jump like they would like to. They are more prone to joint injuries, arthritis, tracheal collapse, chronic bronchitis, and a shortened life span. Still, not all Chihuahuas that look fat are that way from simply overeating. Some disorders, such as heart disease or Cushing's syndrome (see page 87), can cause the appearance of obesity. If you've tried to make your Chihuahua diet and she isn't losing weight, or if she is thin except for her abdomen, you should have your veterinarian check her.

If your Chihuahua checks out normally, it's time for some tough love: a diet! Feed a high-fiber, high-protein diet; several such diets are commercially available, or you can get a recipe from your veterinarian and make your own. Go slowly and feed lots of small meals; remember:

Puppy Food

Puppies should eat puppy food, which is specially formulated for their growth and development needs. Very young puppies should eat about five times a day. In fact, puppies under the age of seven months should eat at least every four hours, except during the night when they should be inactive. You may need to set out a bowl of dry food so they have food available when you're not home. More than for most breeds, it's critically important that young Chihuahuas not go without eating because they can become hypoglycemic. Hypoglycemia occurs when the body runs out of available energy stored as glucogen or as fat, depriving the nervous system of the energy it needs to function properly. Tiny puppies cannot store adequate levels of glucogen or fat to sustain them for very long, especially when they are burning energy rapidly.

Puppies should be fed a puppy food that contains fairly high levels of protein, fat, and complex carbohydrates. These complex carbohydrates, which are often found in starchy foods, are slowly broken down into sugars, allowing them to be available to the dog for a longer period. Puppy foods formulated especially for small breeds should have such ingredients. Simple sugars cause a rapid rise, then drop, in available energy; they are good for a quick source of energy if the dog has already gone too long without eating, but they should be followed immediately by a balanced diet.

Even adult dogs should eat twice a day. You can leave dry food down so the dog can eat at her leisure, but be sure to monitor her food intake each day to make sure she's not off her feed, and monitor her weight to make sure she's not overindulging.

Small dogs have a high metabolic rate and they dissipate heat easily. Going without food for prolonged periods, especially in cold weather or stressful situations, may result in hypoglycemia.

Chihuahua Chow

Many good dog foods are on the market, but you'll find that your dog prefers some more than others. Most people feed a combination of dry and canned foods. Dry food is probably healthier, and it is more economical, but wet food is tastier. Semimoist food has a high sugar content, and is not usually a good choice

for dogs that are predisposed to hypoglycemia. Dog treats and biscuits are good snack foods.

Let your Chihuahua have some say in the food selection process; after all, she has to eat it! But don't let her fool you into running to the store to try yet another delicacy to appease her discriminating palate. Give her a choice, but don't let her learn that if she sticks her nose up at one offering you will replace it with something tastier. That's the recipe for a finicky eater.

One word of warning: One of the great mysteries of canine life is why dogs, who like to drink out of toilets and eat out of garbage cans, and can seemingly do so without ill

effects, can get violently upset stomachs simply from changing from one good food to another. But they do. So when you switch foods, you should do so gradually, mixing in a bit more of the new food for several days until the switch is complete.

Check out the label of the foods you're considering. A good rule of thumb is that four of the first six ingredients should be meat-based. Keep in mind that because the ingredients in canned foods are diluted with water you can't directly compare their percentages to those of dry foods. It's easiest to compare foods of similar moisture contact. The components that vary most among foods are protein and fat.

Protein

Protein percentage should be one of the first things you look for on a label. Most high quality foods are high in protein, and they get that protein from meat rather than plant sources. Animal-derived protein is higher quality and more highly digestible than plant-derived protein; eggs have the highest level of digestible protein of any source. This means that two foods with identical protein percentages can differ in the nutritional level of protein according to the protein's source. Protein is essential for growth and maintenance of bones and muscles, including vital muscles such as the cardiac muscle. Protein is also important for the production of infection-fighting antibodies. Active, growing dogs need higher protein levels. It was once thought that older dogs should be fed low-protein diets in order to avoid kidney problems, but it is now known that high-protein diets do not cause kidney failure. In fact, high-quality protein is essential to dogs with compromised kidney function. Such dogs should have reduced phosphorous levels, however, and special diets are available that satisfy these requirements.

Fat

Fat is the calorie-rich component of foods, and most dogs prefer the taste of foods with higher fat content. Fat is necessary to good health, providing energy and aiding in the transport of important vitamins. Dogs deficient in fat (usually from diets containing less than 5% dry matter fat) may have sparse, dry coats and scaly skin. Excessive fat intake can cause obesity and appetite reduction, creating a deficiency in other nutrients. Obese dogs or dogs with pancreatitis or diarrhea should be fed a low-fat food.

What About Raw?

Some people prefer to feed their dogs a BARF (Bones And Raw Food) diet, with the idea that such a diet better emulates that of a wild dog. They feed raw, meaty bones along with vegetables. Although dogs have better resistance to bacterial food poisoning than do humans, such diets have occasionally been associated with food poisoning, often from salmonella, in dogs. Commercially available meats may be awash in contaminated liquids. Veterinary nutritionists advise that if you do feed raw meat, do not feed ground meat, and seer the meat to kill bacteria on the surface, which is where most pathogens are found.

Advocates of home-prepared diets claim cleaner teeth, fresher breath, better skin, increased vigor, and decreased incidence of bloat. Detractors warn of tooth fractures, intestinal perforations and impactions, pancreatitis, eclampsia, fever, and toxemia. One of the few studies done to analyze the nutritional content of homemade raw diets made to recipe specifications, found the three diets they examined

Food Allergies

Food allergies afflict some dogs, with symptoms ranging from diarrhea to itchy skin and ears. If you suspect that your dog has a food allergy, consult your veterinarian about an elimination diet. This means that you start with a bland diet consisting of ingredients your dog has never eaten before. Lamb and rice foods used to be vigorously promoted as hypoallergenic, but because a dog is now likely to have eaten lamb previously, that is no longer true. Your veterinarian can suggest sources of protein, such as venison, duck, or rabbit, that your dog will probably not have eaten previously. You may have to keep the dog on this diet for at least a month, withholding treats, pills, and even toys that might be creating an allergic response. If the symptoms disappear, then ingredients are added back to the diet gradually, or a novel commercial diet is tried. Alternatively, you can feed a special diet made with proteins having such a low molecular weight that they are essentially too small to cause allergic responses. It may take a lot of experimentation, but a healthy and happy dog will be well worth it.

had various nutrient deficiencies and vitamin and mineral excesses. They had particularly high Vitamin D and were deficient in sodium and phosphorus, with abnormal calcium to phosphorus ratios that can lead to hyperparathyroidism. No controlled studies have been performed to compare health and longevity in dogs fed home-prepared or raw diets to those fed commercial prepared diets. No doubt long-lived dogs have thrived on both types—just as humans manage to thrive on a variety of diets.

She Ate What?

Dogs can eat a variety of strange things. Some dogs have abnormal desires to ingest nonedible substances, including wood, fabric, or soil. Talk to your veterinarian about possible health problems that could contribute to these specific hungers, and about possible problems that could result from eating these items. The most common and seemingly appalling non-food item eaten by dogs is their own feces. This habit, called coprophagia, has been blamed on boredom, stress, hunger, poor nutrition, and excessively rich nutrition, but none of these has proved a completely satisfactory explanation. Food additives are available that make the stool less savory, and you can also try adding hot pepper to it, but a determined dog will not be deterred and the best cure is immediate removal of all feces. Many puppies experiment with stool-eating but grow out of it. Many dogs relish this "treat" for their entire lives, however. Don't be too appalled if yours is one of them; it is a common and perhaps natural behavior of dogs. Just don't share your toothbrush!

Food That Can Kill

Feeding a dog doesn't require military discipline. For most dogs, a few snacks or table scraps won't hurt; in fact, they may be healthy. But be careful when feeding human foods to dogs, especially to little dogs. Also be aware that some human foods can be poisonous to dogs.

✔ Chocolate contains a substance that dogs can't handle called theobromine. Baker's chocolate is particularly high in theobromine; a half ounce of it could kill a 4-pound (1.8-kg) Chihuahua.

✔ Xylitol, an artificial sweetener often used in sugarless gum and candy, can cause hypoglycemia and death.

✔ Onions, and to a lesser extent, garlic, can also be deadly to small dogs. They contain a substance that breaks down red blood cells; if your Chihuahua eats a whole onion it could cause sudden anemia and even death.

✔ Raisins and grapes have been associated with sudden kidney failure and death in some dogs.

✔ Anything that contains drugs, including alcohol and caffeine, is off-limits to dogs in general, and tiny dogs in particular.

✔ Acetaminophen (Tylenol) can cause irreperable liver damage and even death in dogs, especially small dogs.

✔ Bones, too, should generally be kept away from dogs. Small fish and chicken bones can splinter, their sharp ends piercing the digestive tract; larger bones can still be swallowed and cause intestinal obstructions. They also commonly cause broken teeth, particularly the large carnassial tooth.

Mealtime is a major event in a dog's life. Make it pleasant, but remember: What you put in front of your Chihuahua will affect not only her momentary enjoyment, but her long-term health.

TIP

Water

✔ Keep your dog's water bowl filled and clean.

✔ Empty, scrub, and refill the water bowl daily; merely topping it off gives algae and bacteria a chance to multiply.

✔ Most dogs, especially sick ones, appreciate ice cubes added to the water.

AN OUNCE OF PREVENTION

Preventive medicine encompasses accident prevention, contagious disease prevention, parasite control, and health monitoring. Overseeing your Chihuahua's good health is a team effort directed by your veterinarian but undertaken by you. Choose your veterinarian carefully, and take your duties seriously.

The Good Doctor

When choosing your veterinarian, consider availability, emergency arrangements, costs, facilities, and ability to communicate. You and your veterinarian will form a partnership that will work together to protect your Chihuahua's health, so your rapport with your veterinarian is very important. Your veterinarian should listen to your observations, and should explain to you exactly what is happening with your Chihuahua.

When you take your Chihuahua to the veterinary clinic, hold her on leash, on your lap, or in a carrier; if you think your dog may have a contagious illness, inform the clinic beforehand so that you can use another entrance. Your veterinarian will be appreciative if your Chihuahua is clean and under control during the examination. Warn your veterinarian if

you think there is any chance that your dog may bite.

Don't wait until your dog is ill to find a veterinarian. It is best to get to know one another under less stressful circumstances. Establish a working relationship with your veterinarian before calling with an emergency in the middle of the night!

Your veterinarian cannot be at your side at all times, nor are veterinarians infallible. As a dog owner, it's your responsibility to learn about dog health and medicine because ultimately the ability to recognize problems, and the decision to take your dog to the veterinarian, seek a second opinion, or choose between aggressive treatment and euthanasia, rests with you. Large Internet veterinary sites from reputable sources can be a good source of information, as can veterinary books aimed at pet owners.

Give It Your Best Shot

Without well-timed vaccinations, your Chihuahua can be vulnerable to deadly communicable diseases. Your pup received her early immunity through her dam's colostrum during the first few days of nursing. As long as she still has that immunity, any vaccinations you give her won't provide sufficient immunity. But after several weeks, that immunity begins to decrease. As her immunity falls, both the chance of a vaccination being effective and the chance of getting a communicable disease rise. The problem is that immunity diminishes at different times in different dogs. So starting at around six weeks of age, a series of vaccinations is given to catch the time when they will be effective while leaving as little unprotected time as possible. During this time of uncertainty it's best not to take your puppy to places where unvaccinated dogs may congregate. Some deadly viruses, such as parvovirus, can remain in the soil for six months after an infected dog has shed virus in its feces there.

Vaccinations are divided into core vaccines—which are advisable for all dogs—and noncore vaccines—which are advisable only for some dogs. Core vaccines are those for rabies, distemper, parvovirus, and hepatitis (using the CAV-2 vaccine, not the CAV-1, which can cause adverse reactions and is still sold by some feed stores). Noncore vaccines include those for leptospirosis, tracheobronchitis, and Lyme disease.

Your veterinarian can advise you if your dog's lifestyle and environment put her at risk for these diseases. Remember, more is not better!

A sample core vaccination protocol for puppies suggests giving a three-injection series at least three weeks apart, with each injection containing distemper, parvovirus, adenovirus 2 (CAV-2), and parainfluenza (CPIV). The series should not end before 12 weeks of age. A booster is given one year later, and then boosters are given every three years. Rabies should be given at 16 weeks of age, with boosters at one to three year intervals according to local law.

Leptospirosis vaccine is the vaccination most likely to cause adverse reactions, especially in very young or very small dogs, and for that reason many veterinarians elect to omit it from the initial vaccinations. This is especially true if the dog does not walk in wooded areas or drink out of puddles where wild animals could have shed the bacteria.

Many owners of Chihuahua puppies object to the idea that their tiny puppies receive the same dosage of vaccine as do large breed puppies, and some even split the dose in half. This is not good practice. The amount of vaccine has been titrated to elicit an immune reaction, and just as infection by a virus doesn't depend on how large the dog is, neither does immunity.

Some proponents of natural rearing condemn vaccinations and refuse to use them. They use homeopathic nosodes instead, and point to the fact that their dogs don't get sick as proof that they work. However, no controlled study has ever supported the effectiveness of nosodes, and these people's good fortune is probably the result of herd immunity; that is, as long as most other dogs are vaccinated they probably never come in contact with the infectious agents.

Internal Parasites

Another major area of preventive health care is external and internal parasite prevention. (External parasites were discussed on page 51.) Internal parasites can rob your dog of vital nutrients, good health, and sometimes, even a long life. The most common internal parasites invade the heart or intestines.

Heartworms

Heartworms are deadly parasites carried by mosquitoes. Wherever mosquitoes are present, dogs should be on heartworm prevention. Several effective types of heartworm preventive are available, with some also preventing many other types of worms. Some require daily administration, while others require only monthly or twice-yearly administration. The monthly type is most popular and actually has a wider margin of safety and protection than the daily type. It doesn't stay in the dog's system for a month, but instead, acts on a particular stage in the heartworm's development. Giving the drug each month prevents any heartworms from ever maturing. In warm areas your dog may need to be on prevention year-round, but in milder climates your dog may need to use prevention only during the warmer months. Your veterinarian can advise you.

If you forget to give the heartworm preventive as prescribed, your dog may get heartworms. A dog with suspected heartworms should not be given the daily preventive because a fatal reaction could occur. The most common way of checking for heartworms is to check the blood for circulating microfilarae (the immature form of heartworms), but this method may fail to detect the presence of adult heartworms in as many as 20 percent of all tested dogs. More accurate is an occult heartworm test, which detects antigens to heartworms in the blood. With either test, heartworms will not be detectable until nearly seven months after the dog is infected. Heartworms can be eradicated, but the treatment is comparatively expensive and not without risks, although a less risky treatment has recently become available. If untreated, heartworms can kill your dog.

Intestinal Parasites

Intestinal parasites are common, especially where large groups of dogs commingle. Left untreated, worms can cause vomiting, diarrhea, dull coat, listlessness, and anemia. Don't be tempted to pick up some worm medication and worm your dog yourself; over-the-counter dewormers are largely ineffective and often more

dangerous than those available through your veterinarian. Dogs should be wormed only when they have been tested and shown to have worms, and only for the particular type of worm they have. And no, garlic does not get rid of worms.

Some heartworm preventives also prevent most types of intestinal worms (but not tapeworms). Protozoan parasites, such as coccidia and especially, *Giardia,* can cause chronic or intermittent diarrhea. Your veterinarian can diagnose them with a stool specimen and prescribe appropriate medication.

Tapeworms are the easiest worms for you to detect at home because you can see their long flat segments wriggling around on fresh stools, or you can find their dried up segments (resembling grains of rice) around the dog's anus. They're pretty disgusting, and certainly irritating to the dog, although actually not as debilitating as many of the other worms. They also signal that your dog has fleas. Dogs get tapeworms from eating fleas that carry tapeworms; dogs can also get another type of tapeworm from eating raw rabbits, but chances are your Chihuahua isn't doing that much rabbit catching. So if you want to do away with tapeworms, do away with fleas.

Too Much of a Good Thing— Spaying or Neutering

As your puppy grows up, one of the decisions you'll be faced with is when—or if—to spay or neuter your dog. As a responsible dog owner, you should not want to add to the overpopulation of dogs.

Even though you may be adamant that you can keep your dog from having an unplanned litter, it takes diligence and security measures to

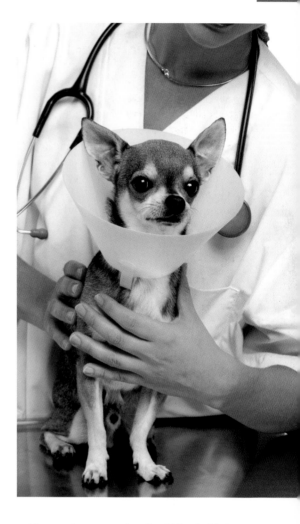

ensure that a mating does not take place. Living with a dog in heat can be difficult. Most dogs go into heat twice a year; it lasts about three weeks, during which time she has a bloody discharge that can stain your rugs and furniture. Very often, because of their small size and clean habits, Chihuahuas can be in season some time before you notice—leading to the possibility of an unplanned pregnancy. If you own both an intact male and female, the male may drive you crazy with his panting and whining.

Intact males are more likely to urine mark inside the house. Again, castration is the convenient option.

Both surgeries are very safe, although as with any surgery, some slight risk is involved. There are also long term health pros and cons for both procedures. For females, spaying before the first heat greatly decreases the risk of breast cancer. This is the most common tumor of female dogs. Spaying also removes possibility of pyometra, a potentially fatal infection of the uterus.

Spaying is also associated with an increased risk of urinary incontinence, which occurs in 5 to 20 percent of spayed females, but it's far less common in smaller breeds. Several other concerns related to spaying are also not common in small breeds. Overall, it is probably best to spay bitches between 3 months of age and their first heat—sometime around 4 to 5 months of age.

With castration (neutering), there are also pros and cons. Castration removes the risk of testicular cancer. It reduces the risk of an enlarged prostate, which occurs in about 80 percent of intact male dogs over the age of 6 years. The condition can be treated with (among other things) castration. Castration has some cons, though, but again, most are more likely in large breeds.

Like spaying, castration should be decided on a case by case basis. Many dog parks, doggy daycares, and camps won't allow dogs to attend if they have not been castrated. If you castrate your dog, you should probably have it done around 6 months of age, before he starts urine marking. Once that becomes a habit, he may continue to mark even after castration.

HOW-TO: GIVE YOUR

One of the most important things you can do for your dog's health is to get to know her body and behavior when she's healthy. You do this by giving her a monthly or even weekly five-minute checkup, examining

✔ the mouth for reddened, bleeding, swollen or pale gums, loose teeth, ulcers of the tongue or gums, or bad breath.

✔ the eyes for discharge, cloudiness, or discolored "whites."

✔ the ears for foul odor, redness, discharge, or crusted tips.

✔ the nose for thickened or colored discharge.

✔ the skin for parasites, hair loss, crusts, red spots, or lumps.

✔ the feet for cuts, abrasions, split nails, bumps, or misaligned toes.

✔ the bones and muscles for asymmetry.

✔ the mammary glands or testicles for lumps.

✔ the penis or vulva for excessive discharge.

✔ the abdomen for swelling or lumps.

You should also be on the lookout every day for signs of
✔ behavioral change
✔ lethargy
✔ loss of balance
✔ incoordination
✔ circling
✔ difficulty breathing
✔ gagging
✔ weight change
✔ change in appetite or water consumption
✔ abnormal urination or urine
✔ incontinence
✔ black or bloody stool
✔ sores
✔ lameness

Temperature and Pulse

To take your dog's temperature, lubricate a rectal thermometer (preferably the digital type), insert it about 1 inch (2.5 cm) into the dog's anus, and leave it for about two minutes. Normal temperature for a Chihuahua ranges from 100 to 102.5°F (37.8–38.7°C). Call your veterinarian if the temperature is over 104°F (40°C).

A good place to check the pulse is on the femoral artery, located inside the rear leg, where the thigh meets the abdomen. Normal pulse rates range from 80 to 160 beats per minute in an awake Chihuahua, with strong and fairly regular beats.

CHIHUAHUA A CHECKUP

The Health Chart

Make several copies of this chart and keep a record of your dog's home exams.

Date: _____

Temperature: _____ Pulse: _____

First consider your dog's general behavior. Is your dog
Restless? _____
Tired? _____
Irritable? _____
Weak? _____
Confused? _____
Limping? _____
Acting dizzy? _____
Bumping into things? _____
Eating a lot less than usual? _____
Eating a lot more than usual? _____
Drinking a lot more than usual? _____
Urinating a lot more than usual? _____
Having difficulty urinating? _____
Having accidents in the house? _____
Having diarrhea? _____
Vomiting or trying to vomit? _____
Coughing? _____
Breathing more rapidly than usual? _____

Now give your dog's body a more thorough exam.

Check the nose for:
Thick or colored discharge _____
Sudden loss of color _____
Sores or crustiness _____

Check the mouth for:
Bad breath _____
Soreness _____
Loose teeth _____
Dirty teeth _____
Gum color (anything but pink requires a
   veterinary exam):
   pink (good) _____   almost white _____
   bright red _____   yellowish _____
   bluish _____   red spots _____
Swollen gums _____
Bleeding _____
Sores _____
Growths _____

Check the eyes for:
Watery tears _____
Thick discharge _____
Squinting _____
Pawing at an eye _____
Swollen eye _____
Cloudy or dull surface _____
Red sclera ("whites") _____
Unequal-sized pupils _____

Check the ears for:
Bad smell _____
Redness inside _____
Lots of black ear wax _____
Scabby ear tips _____
Head shaking _____
Head carried tilted _____
Ear scratching _____
Painfulness _____

Check the feet for:
Cuts _____
Split nails _____
Long nails _____
Swollen toes _____
Toes out of alignment _____

Check the skin for:
Parasites _____
Black "flea dirt" _____
Hair loss _____
Scabs _____
Red spots _____
Lumps _____
Sores _____

Check the anal and genital regions for:
Swelling _____
Redness _____
Discharge _____
Dog constantly licking at its anus _____
Dog scooting rear end on ground _____
Black or bloody stool _____
Bloody urine _____
Signs of diarrhea _____

A POUND OF CURE

Like people, dogs often feel under the weather. Unlike people, they have a hard time telling you where it hurts. So you have to be part detective and part doctor to know what your dog is trying to tell you about how she feels.

Signs of Sickness

Lethargy

Lack of energy or interest often signals that your dog isn't feeling well. First check her gum color to make sure her circulation is adequate; gums should be pink, without red spots, and when you press on a spot the pink color should return within a couple of seconds. If this is not the case, call the veterinarian immediately.

Fever is another common cause of lethargic behavior. Take your dog's temperature; if it's over 102.5°F (38.7°C), then she has a fever. If it's over 104°F (40°C), call the veterinarian immediately.

Pain can also cause lethargy. Carefully feel your dog all over her body, pressing gently on her limbs, teeth, abdomen, back, and neck. Depending on her reaction, you may need to make an appointment with the veterinarian.

Many internal disorders can cause lethargic behavior. The only way to detect them is with professional testing. For example, blood tests can detect problems in many internal organs that could be causing your dog to feel sick. Radiographs or ultrasounds could detect internal growths or blockages that could be causing illness. In most cases, lethargic behavior calls for a visit to the veterinarian.

Loss of Appetite

Loss of appetite often occurs along with lethargic behavior, so the first steps to take are to perform the same checks you would do in cases of lethargy. Try a different diet; like people, dogs sometimes get tired of eating a certain food. And like people, dogs can develop aversions to foods they ate just before becoming nauseated. You may have to cook for your dog and spoil her a little bit. Usually, dogs prefer food that is warmed to body temperature; an exception, however, is a nauseated dog, for whom the increased aroma can increase the feeling of nausea. So try both warm and cold foods, as well as bland and rich flavors. If your dog continues to have a noticeably smaller

appetite, you may need to return to the veterinarian for more testing; loss of appetite in a dog that previously had a good appetite can be a sign of a serious problem.

Diarrhea

Diarrhea can result from overexcitement or nervousness, a change in diet or water, sensitivity to certain foods, overeating, intestinal parasites, viral or bacterial infections, or ingestion of toxic substances. Bloody diarrhea, or diarrhea combined with vomiting, fever, or other signs of toxicity, or diarrhea that lasts for more than a day should not be allowed to continue without veterinary advice. Some of these could be symptomatic of potentially fatal disorders.

Less severe diarrhea can be treated at home by serving a bland diet consisting of rice, tapioca, or cooked macaroni, along with cottage cheese or tofu for protein for several days.

Vomiting

Vomiting is a common occurrence that may or may not indicate a serious problem.

✔ Vomiting after eating grass is usually of no great concern. Vomiting immediately after meals could indicate an obstruction of the esophagus.

✔ Repeated vomiting could indicate that the dog has eaten spoiled food, undigestible objects, or may have stomach illness. Veterinary advice should be sought. Meanwhile, withhold food (or feed as directed for diarrhea) and restrict water.

✔ Consult your veterinarian immediately if your dog vomits a foul substance resembling fecal matter (indicating a blockage in the intestinal tract), blood (partially digested blood resembles coffee grounds), or if there is projectile or continued vomiting.

✔ Sporadic vomiting with poor appetite and generally poor condition could indicate internal parasites or a more serious internal disease that should also be checked by your veterinarian.

Coughing

Any persistent cough should be checked by your veterinarian. Coughing irritates the throat and can lead to secondary infections or other more serious problems if allowed to continue unchecked. It can also be miserable for the dog. Allergies, foreign bodies, pneumonia, parasites, tracheal collapse, tumors, and especially, kennel cough and heart disease, can all cause coughing.

Kennel cough is a highly communicable airborne disease caused by several different infectious agents. It is characterized by a gagging cough arising about a week after exposure. Inoculations are available and are a good idea if you plan to have your dog around other dogs at training classes or while being boarded.

Heart disease can cause coughing, most often following exercise or in the evening. Affected dogs will often lie down and point their nose in the air in order to breathe better. Drug treatment is essential.

Tracheal collapse is described on page 82.

Urinating Abnormally

If your dog has difficulty or pain urinating, or urinates suddenly and often but in small amounts, or passes cloudy or bloody urine, she may be suffering from a problem of the bladder, urethra, or prostate. Urinalysis and a rectal exam by your veterinarian are necessary to diagnose the exact nature of the problem. Bladder infections must be treated promptly to prevent the infection from reaching the kidneys. Dribbling of urine during sleep, most often by spayed females, can indicate a hormonal problem.

Blockage of urine can result in death. Inability to urinate requires immediate emergency veterinary attention.

Kidney disease, ultimately leading to kidney failure, is one of the most common ailments of older dogs. The earliest signs are usually increased drinking and urinating. Although the excessive urination may cause problems keeping your house clean or your night's sleep intact, never try to restrict water from a dog with kidney disease. Increased urination can

also be a sign of diabetes or a urinary tract infection. Your veterinarian can discover the cause with some simple tests, and each of these conditions can be treated. For kidney disease, a special diet can slow the progression.

Prostate disease: In males, infections of the prostate gland can lead to repeated urinary tract infections, and even painful defecation or blood and pus in the urine. Castration and long-term antibiotic therapy are the best therapies.

Licking the Anus or Scooting

Constant licking of the anus or scooting of the rear along the ground are characteristic signs of anal sac impaction. Dogs have two anal sacs that are normally emptied by rectal

The Medicine Chest
✔ rectal thermometer
✔ scissors
✔ tweezers
✔ sterile gauze dressings
✔ self-adhesive bandage (such as Vet-Wrap)
✔ instant cold compress
✔ antidiarrhea medication
✔ ophthalmic ointment
✔ soap
✔ antiseptic skin ointment
✔ hydrogen peroxide
✔ clean sponge
✔ pen light
✔ syringe
✔ towel
✔ first aid instructions
✔ veterinarian and emergency clinic numbers
✔ poison control center number

pressure during defecation. Their musky-smelling contents may also be forcibly ejected when a dog is extremely frightened. Sometimes they fail to empty properly, so they become impacted or infected. This is more common in obese dogs, dogs with allergies or seborrhea, and dogs that seldom have firm stools, but it can happen to any dog. Impacted sacs cause extreme discomfort and can become infected; eventually they can swell so much they rupture, with the contents coming through the dog's skin next to his anus. Treatment consists of manually emptying the sacs, sometimes refilling them with an antibiotic ointment, and giving the dog oral antibiotics.

Itching

Itching can be caused by external parasites, allergies or skin problems (see page 51 for a discussion of these conditions).

In Case of Emergency

Even experienced dog owners have a difficult time deciding what constitutes a true emergency; when in doubt, err on the side of caution and call the emergency clinic or your veterinarian for their opinion.

Be Prepared

Because there are no paramedics for dogs, you must assume the role of paramedic and ambulance driver in case of an emergency. Now is the time to prepare for these life-saving roles.

1. Know the phone number and location of the emergency veterinarian in your area.

2. Keep the number next to the phone; don't rely on your memory during an emergency situation.

3. Study the emergency procedures described in this chapter, and keep this guide handy. Misplaced instructions can result in the loss of critical time.

4. Always keep enough fuel in your car to make it to the emergency clinic without stopping for gas.

5. Finally, stay calm. It will help you help your dog, and will help your dog stay calm as well. A calm dog is less likely to go into shock.

✔ Make sure you and the dog are in a safe location.

✔ Make sure breathing passages are open. Remove any collar and check the mouth and throat.

✔ Move the dog as little and as gently as possible.

✔ Control any bleeding.

✔ Check breathing, pulse, and consciousness.

✔ Check for signs of shock (very pale gums, weakness, unresponsiveness, faint pulse, shivering). Treat by keeping the dog warm and calm.

✔ Never use force or do anything that causes extreme discomfort.

✔ Never remove an impaled object (unless it is blocking the airway).

For the following situations, administer first aid and seek veterinary attention. Situations not described in this list can usually be treated with the same first aid as for humans. In all cases, the best advice is to seek the opinion of a veterinarian.

Poisoning

Signs of poisoning vary according to the type of poison, but commonly include vomiting, convulsions, staggering, and collapse. In most cases, home treatment is not advisable. If in doubt about whether poison was ingested,

call the veterinarian anyway. If possible, bring the poison and its container with you to the veterinarian.

Call the veterinarian or poison control hotline and give as much information as possible. Induce vomiting (except in the cases outlined on page 78) by giving either hydrogen peroxide (mixed 1:1 with water), salt water, or dry mustard and water. Treat for shock and get to the veterinarian at once. Be prepared for convulsions or respiratory distress.

Medications

✔ When giving pills, open your dog's mouth and place the pill well to the back of the mouth. Close the mouth and gently stroke the throat until your dog swallows. Pre-wetting capsules or covering them with cream cheese or some other food helps prevent capsules from sticking to the tongue or roof of the mouth.

✔ For liquid medicine, tilt the head back, keep the dog's mouth almost (but not quite tightly) closed, and place the liquid in the pouch of the cheek. Then hold the mouth closed until the dog swallows.

✔ Always give the full course of medications prescribed by your veterinarian.

✔ Don't give your dog human medications unless you have been directed to do so by your veterinarian. Some medications for humans have no effect upon dogs, and some can have a very detrimental effect.

Do not induce vomiting if the poison was an acid, alkali, petroleum product, solvent, cleaner, tranquilizer, or if a sharp object was swallowed; also do not induce vomiting if the dog is severely depressed, convulsing, comatose, or if more than two hours have passed since ingestion. If the dog is not convulsing or unconscious, dilute the poison by giving milk, vegetable oil, or egg whites. Activated charcoal can adsorb many toxins. Baking soda or milk of magnesia can be given for ingested acids, and vinegar or lemon juice for ingested alkalis.

Two of the most common and life-threatening poisons eaten by dogs are Warfarin (rodent poison) and especially, ethylene glycol (antifreeze). Veterinary treatment must be obtained within two to four hours of ingestion of even tiny amounts if the dog's life is to be saved. *Do not wait for symptoms.* By the time symptoms of antifreeze poisoning are evident it is usually too late to save the dog.

Seizures

A dog undergoing a seizure may drool, become stiff, or have uncontrollable muscle spasms.

Wrap the dog securely in a blanket to prevent her from injuring herself on furniture or stairs. Remove other dogs from the area (they may attack the convulsing dog). Never put your hands, or anything, in a convulsing dog's mouth. Treat for shock. Make note of all characteristics and sequences of seizure activity, which can help to diagnose the cause. Take the dog to the veterinarian.

Allergic Reaction

Insect stings are the most common cause of extreme reactions. Swelling around the nose and throat can block the airway. Other possible reactions include restlessness, vomiting, diarrhea, seizures, and collapse. If any of these symptoms occur, immediate veterinary attention will probably be necessary.

Bleeding

Consider wounds to be an emergency if they bleed profusely, are extremely deep, or are open to the chest cavity, abdominal cavity, or head.

Control massive bleeding first. Cover the wound with clean dressing and apply pressure; apply more dressings over the others until

bleeding stops. Also elevate the wound site, and apply a cold pack to the site. If the wound is on an extremity, apply pressure to the closest pressure point as follows:

✔ For a front leg: inside of the front leg just above the elbow.

✔ For a rear leg: inside of the thigh where the femoral artery crosses the thigh bone.

✔ For the tail: underside of tail close to where it joins the body.

Use a tourniquet only in life-threatening situations and when all other attempts have failed. Check for signs of shock.

Sucking chest wounds: Place a sheet of plastic or other nonporous material over the hole and bandage it to make as airtight a seal as possible.

Abdominal wounds: Place a warm, wet, sterile dressing over any protruding internal organs; cover with a bandage or towel. Do not attempt to push organs back into the dog.

Head wounds: Apply gentle pressure to control bleeding. Monitor for loss of consciousness or shock and treat accordingly.

Take the dog to the veterinarian.

Burns

Deep burns, characterized by charred or pearly white skin, with deeper layers of tissue exposed, are serious.

Cool the burned area with cool packs, towels soaked in water, or by immersing it in cold water. If over 50 percent of the dog is burned, do not immerse as this increases likelihood of shock. Cover with a clean bandage or towel to avoid contamination. Do not apply pressure; do not apply ointments. Monitor for shock. Take the dog to the veterinarian.

Electrical Shock

A dog that chews on an electric cord may collapse and have burns inside her mouth.

Before touching the dog, disconnect the plug or cut power; if that cannot be done immediately, use a *wooden* pencil, spoon, or broom handle to knock the cord away from the dog. Keep the dog warm and treat for shock. Monitor breathing and heartbeat. Take the dog to the veterinarian.

Heatstroke

Rapid, loud breathing; abundant thick saliva, bright red mucous membranes, and high rectal temperature are earlier signs of heatstroke. Later signs include unsteadiness, diarrhea, and coma.

Wet the dog down and place her in front of a fan. If this is not possible immerse the dog in cool water. *Do not plunge the dog in ice water;* the resulting constriction of peripheral blood vessels can make the situation worse. Offer small amounts of water for drinking. You must lower your dog's body temperature quickly, but do not lower it below 100°F (37.8°C). Stop cooling the dog when the temperature reaches 103°F (39.4°C). Take the dog to the veterinarian.

Hypothermia

Shivering, cold feeling, and sluggishness are signs that the dog has become excessively chilled. Later signs include a very low—under 95°F (35°C)—body temperature, slow pulse and breathing rates, and coma.

Warm the dog gradually. Wrap her in a blanket (preferably one that has been warmed in the dryer). Place plastic bottles filled with hot water outside the blankets, not touching the dog. You can also place a plastic tarp over the blanket, making sure the dog's head is not covered. Monitor the temperature. Stop warming when the temperature reaches 101°F (38.3°C). Take the dog to the veterinarian.

Hypoglycemia (Low Blood Sugar)

A dog with low blood sugar may appear disoriented or weak, may stagger, and perhaps appear blind. Her muscles may twitch. Later stages lead to convulsions, coma, and death.

Give food, honey, or syrup mixed with warm water. If the dog cannot eat, rub syrup on its gums. Follow with a high-protein meal. Take the dog to the veterinarian.

When in doubt about any of your dog's symptoms, call your veterinarian!

Every breed of dog has certain health problems that occur in that breed more often than in other breeds. The list for some breeds is long; the list for Chihuahuas is short. But even Chihuahuas have special concerns every Chihuahua owner should know about.

✔ **Open fontanel,** or molera, refers to a soft spot on the head where the bones of the skull have failed to fuse. This is a typical trait of Chihuahuas and a small molera has no detrimental effect on health. A large molera can

render the brain susceptible to trauma from blows to the head; after all, the skull is there to protect the brain. While all Chihuahuas should be protected from head injuries, a dog with a large molera must be guarded with even more vigilance.

✔ **Patellar luxation** occurs when the dog's patella, or kneecap, slips out of the groove it normally rests in along the front of the femur (thigh) bone, either because the groove is too shallow or the muscles attached to the patella are too tight. When

it pops out of place the dog needs to straighten her leg for it to pop back in, so the dog usually hops a couple of steps before it slips back in place and she can trot normally again. In severe cases it won't pop back in unless a person manipulates it back into place. Mild cases may be managed by keeping the dog's weight down and building up her muscles, but even then they often get worse and eventually become so bad that surgery is needed for the dog's comfort.

✔ **Tracheal collapse** occurs when the cartilage of the trachea, or windpipe, is weak. The weakened area can be affected by other factors such as obesity, airborne irritants, and coughing so that the tracheal rings collapse. This causes the trachea to flatten, obstructing the airway. The condition occurs most often in middle-aged or older dogs; the major sign is coughing. Affected dogs should wear harnesses rather than collars, and be kept away from anything that could cause irritation of their airways. Severe cases may need surgery.

✔ **Pulmonic stenosis** is a condition of the heart in which the passage is abnor-

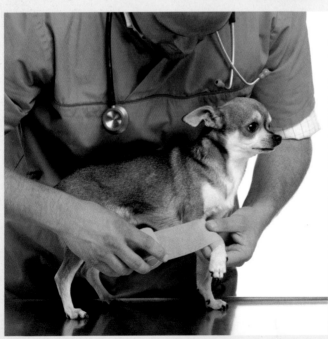

mally narrow between the heart's right ventricle and the pulmonary valve leading eventually to the lungs. This causes the heart to work harder to move blood through it, eventually causing the right ventricle to become thickened and in some cases, leading to heart failure. Dogs with heart failure may be easily tired or may even faint when exercising. Your veterinarian can do an initial check, but a complete exam and any treatment should be performed by a veterinary cardiologist.

✔ **Hydrocephalus** occurs when the open spaces of the brain, called ventricles, become overfilled with cerebrospinal fluid, which in turn exerts pressure on the brain and eventually causes brain damage. Outward signs sometimes include a large, domed skull and an open fontanel, which are traits often seen in perfectly normal as well as hydrocephalic Chihuahuas. Some affected dogs have widely set eyes that are turned outward so they look to the sides more than normal. More definite signs include seizures, slowed learning, incoordination, involuntary eye movements, and visual problems. Your veterinarian can suggest more definitive tests and give you information about treatment options.

✔ **Hypoplasia of dens** occurs when part of one of the vertebrae in the neck is abnormal, which allows the atlas and axis neck vertebrae to slip up and down relative to one another, compressing the spinal cord as it runs between them. Surgery may be needed to prevent pain and even paralysis.

✔ **Hypoglycemia** occurs when the body depletes its supply of available glucose, depriving the brain of energy. It is described in more detail on page 80; emergency treatment is described on page 76.

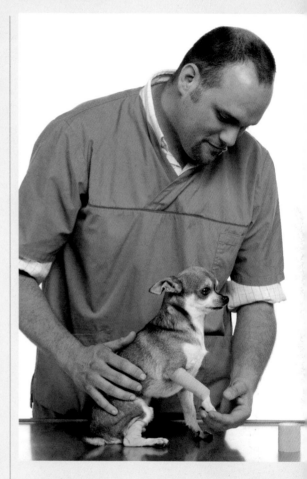

✔ **Cryptorchidism** refers to the failure of one or both testicles to descend into the scrotum in male dogs. Retained testicles do not produce viable sperm and are also more likely to become cancerous, so most veterinarians suggest removing them. The condition is more common in small breeds.

You and your Chihuahua have a lifetime of experiences to share. Your life may change dramatically in the years to come: marriage, divorce, new baby, new home—for better or worse, your Chi will still depend on you and still love you. Always remember the promise you made before you made the commitment to share your life: to keep your interest in your dog and care for her every day of her life with as much love and enthusiasm as you did the first day she arrived home.

Your Chihuahua will change through the years. The Chihuahua's legendary longevity sometimes misleads owners into expecting their Chihuahuas to live forever. But one day you will look at your youngster and be shocked to discover that her face has silvered and her gait has stiffened. She sleeps longer and more soundly than she used to, and she's slower to get going. She is less eager to play and more content to lie in the sun. Yet the older Chihuahua, her eyes often hazy from cataracts, her gait stiff, and her face gray, is in the opinion of many Chihuahua lovers the most beautiful Chihuahua of all.

Dogs, like people, age at different rates. Small dogs tend to live longer than large dogs; even so, Chihuahuas typically show definite signs of old age by age ten. The average life span is about 14 years, although many live much longer, and of course, many fail to live that long.

Old Dogs, New Tricks

It is important to keep your dog active, but exercise should be moderated. Walking or even swimming is easier on old joints than running. Mental stimulation is also important. Teaching your old dog a new trick every month is a good way to keep her mind young. A simple game of hide-the-dog-bone-under-the-chair-and-see-if-she-can-find-it is fun, rewarding, and easy on the old dog.

Older dogs may experience hearing or visual loss. Be careful not to startle a dog with impaired senses, as a startled dog could snap in self-defense. The slight haziness that appears in the older dog's pupils is normal and has minimal effect upon vision, but some dogs, especially those with diabetes, may develop cataracts that interfere with vision. These can be removed by a veterinary ophthalmologist if they are severe. Dogs with gradual vision loss can cope well as long as they are kept in familiar surroundings and extra safety precautions are followed.

Some older dogs become cranky and less patient, especially when dealing with puppies or boisterous children. But don't just excuse behavioral changes, especially if sudden, as due simply to aging. They could be symptoms of pain or disease.

Long trips may be grueling, and boarding in a kennel may be upsetting. The immune system may be less effective in older dogs, so it is increasingly important to shield your dog from infectious disease, chilling, overheating, and any stressful conditions.

Senior Diets

Both physical activity and metabolic rates decrease in older animals, so they require fewer calories to maintain their weight. Feeding old dogs like young dogs makes them fat old dogs. Fat dogs have a greater risk of cardiovascular and joint problems. Although most geriatric dogs have a tendency to be overweight, some lose weight and may need to eat puppy food in order to keep the pounds on.

Arthritis

While Chihuahuas of any age enjoy a soft warm bed, such a bed is an absolute necessity for older Chis. Degenerative joint disease (DJD)—more commonly called arthritis—is a common cause of intermittent stiffness and lameness. Conservative treatment of arthritis entails keeping the dog's weight down, attending to injuries, and maintaining a program of exercise. Low-impact exercise such as walking or swimming every other day is best for dogs with signs of arthritis. Newer drugs, such as carprofen, are available from your veterinarian and may help alleviate some of the symptoms of DJD, but they should be used only with careful veterinary supervision.

Some newer drugs and supplements may actually improve the joint:

✔ Polysulfated glycosaminoglycan increases the compressive resilience of cartilage.

✔ Glucosamine stimulates the synthesis of collagen, and may help rejuvenate cartilage to some extent.

✔ Chondroitin sulfate helps to shield cartilage from destructive enzymes.

Older dogs should be fed several small meals instead of one large meal, and should be fed on time. Moistening dry food or feeding canned food can help a dog with dental problems enjoy her meal.

Most senior Chihuahuas do not require a special diet unless they have a particular medical need for it, for example, obesity: low calorie; kidney failure: low phosphorous; heart failure: low sodium.

Geriatric Medicine

The older dog should be seen by her veterinarian at least twice a year. Blood tests can detect early stages of diseases that treatment could cure. Although older dogs present a somewhat greater anesthesia risk, most of this increased risk can be negated by first performing a complete medical workup to screen for problems.

Older dogs tend to have a stronger body odor, but don't just ignore increased odors. They could indicate specific problems, such as periodontal disease, impacted anal sacs, seborrhea, ear infections, or even kidney disease. Any strong odor should be checked by your veterinarian. Like people, dogs lose skin moisture as they age, and though dogs don't have to worry about wrinkles, their skin can become dry and itchy. Regular brushing can help by stimulating oil production.

In general, any ailment that an older dog has is magnified in severity compared to the same symptoms in a younger dog. Some of the more common symptoms and their possible cause in older Chihuahuas include

✔ Diarrhea: kidney or liver disease, pancreatitis
✔ Coughing: heart disease, lung cancer
✔ Difficulty eating: periodontal disease, oral tumors

Cushing's Syndrome

Cushing's syndrome (hyperadrenocorticism) is seen mostly in older dogs, and is characterized by increased drinking and urination, potbellied appearance, symmetrical hair loss on the body, darkened skin, and susceptibility to infections.

✔ Decreased appetite: kidney, liver, or heart disease, pancreatitis, cancer
✔ Increased appetite: diabetes, Cushing's syndrome
✔ Weight loss: heart, liver, or kidney disease, diabetes, cancer
✔ Abdominal distention (gradual): heart or kidney disease, Cushing's syndrome, tumor
✔ Increased urination: diabetes, kidney, or liver disease, cystitis, Cushing's syndrome
✔ Limping: arthritis, cancer
✔ Nasal discharge: tumor, periodontal disease

If you are lucky enough to have an old Chihuahua, you still must accept that the time will come when some disease will strike. Heart disease, kidney failure, or cancer eventually claim most of these senior citizens. Early detection can help delay their effects, but unfortunately, can seldom prevent them ultimately.

The Friend of a Lifetime

Despite the best of care, eventually neither you nor your veterinarian can prevent your cherished friend from succumbing to old age or an incurable illness. It's hard to believe you will have to say good-bye to someone who has been such a focal point of your life—in truth, a real member of your family. That dogs live such

a short time compared to humans is a cruel fact, but one that you must ultimately face.

Euthanasia

Because many terminal illnesses make your dog feel very ill, there may come a point where your desire to keep your friend with you as long as possible may not be the kindest thing for either of you. Euthanasia is a difficult and personal decision that no one wants to make. Consider whether your dog has a reasonable chance of getting better, and how your dog seems to feel. Financial considerations can be a factor if it means going into debt in exchange for just a little while longer. Your own emotional state must also be considered. For every person the ultimate point is different. Most people probably put off doing something for longer than is really the kindest thing because they don't want to act in haste and be haunted by thoughts that just maybe it was a temporary setback. And of course, they put it off because they can't stand the thought of saying good-bye.

We all wish that if our dog has to go, she would fall asleep and never wake up. This, unfortunately, seldom happens. Even when it does, you are left with the regret that you never got to say good-bye. The closest you can come to this is with euthanasia. Euthanasia is painless and involves giving an overdose of an anesthetic. Essentially the dog will fall asleep and die almost instantly. In a very sick dog, because the circulation is compromised, this may take slightly longer, but the dog is unconscious.

If you do decide that euthanasia is the kindest farewell gesture for your beloved friend, discuss with your veterinarian what will happen. You may ask about giving your dog a tranquilizer beforehand, or having the doctor meet you at home. Although it won't be easy, try to remain with your dog so that her last moments will be filled with your love. Try to recall the wonderful times you have shared and realize that however painful losing such a once-in-a-lifetime friend is, it is better than never having had such a partner at all.

Eternally in Your Heart

Many people who regarded their Chihuahua as a member of the family nonetheless feel embarrassed at the grief they feel at its loss, even though this dog has often functioned as a surrogate child, best friend, and confidant. Partnership with a pet can be one of the closest and most stable relationships in many people's lives. Unfortunately, the support from friends that comes with human loss is too often absent with pet loss. There are, however, many people who share your feelings and there are pet bereavement counselors available at many veterinary schools.

After losing such a cherished friend, many people say they will never get another dog. True, no dog will ever take the place of your dog. But you will find that another Chihuahua is a welcome diversion and will help keep you from dwelling on the loss of your first love. True also, by getting another dog you are sentencing yourself to the same grief in another few years, but wouldn't you rather have that than miss out on a second once-in-a-lifetime dog?

The loss of a companion may mark the end of an era for you, a time when you and your Chihuahua grew up or grew old together. But one could scarcely ask for a better life partner than a special Chihuahua. Those who have shared their lives with the world's smallest dogs know that these dogs have the world's biggest hearts.

The Chihuahua AKC Standard of Perfection

General Appearance

A graceful, alert, swift-moving compact little dog with saucy expression, and with terrier-like qualities of temperament.

Size, Proportion, Substance

Weight—A well balanced little dog not to exceed 6 pounds. *Proportion*—The body is off-square; hence, slightly longer when measured from point of shoulder to point of buttocks, than height at the withers. Somewhat shorter bodies are preferred in males. *Disqualification*—Any dog over 6 pounds in weight.

Head

A well rounded "apple dome" skull, with or without molera. *Expression*—Saucy. *Eyes*—Full, round, but not protruding, balanced, set well apart-luminous dark or luminous ruby. Light eyes in blond or white-colored dogs permissible. Blue eyes or a difference in the color of the iris in the two eyes, or two different colors within one iris should be considered a serious fault. *Ears*—Large, erect type ears, held more upright when alert, but flaring to the sides at a 45 degree angle when in repose, giving breadth between the ears. *Stop*—Well defined. When viewed in profile, it forms a near 90 degree angle where muzzle joins skull. *Muzzle*—Moderately short, slightly pointed. Cheeks and jaws lean. *Nose*—Self-colored in blond types, or black. In moles, blues, and chocolates, they are self-colored. In blond types, pink noses permissible. *Bite*—Level or scissors. Overshot or undershot, or any distortion of the bite or jaw,

should be penalized as a serious fault. A missing tooth or two is permissible. *Disqualifications—Broken down or cropped ears.*

Neck, Topline, Body

Neck—Slightly arched, gracefully sloping into lean shoulders. *Topline*—Level. *Body*—Ribs rounded and well sprung (but not too much "barrel-shaped"). *Tail*—Moderately long, carried sickle either up or out, or in a loop over the back with tip just touching the back.(Never tucked between legs.) *Disqualifications—Docked tail, bobtail.*

Forequarters

Shoulders—Lean, sloping into a slightly broadening support above straight forelegs that set well under, giving free movement at the elbows. Shoulders should be well up, giving balance and soundness, sloping into a level back (never down or low). This gives a well developed chest and strength of forequarters. *Feet*—A small, dainty foot with toes well split up but not spread, pads cushioned. (Neither the hare nor the cat foot.) Dewclaws may be removed. *Pasterns*—Strong.

Hindquarters

Muscular, with hocks well apart, neither out nor in, well let down, firm and sturdy. *Angulation*—Should equal that of forequarters. The feet are as in front. Dewclaws may be removed.

Coat

In the *Smooth Coats*, the coat should be of soft texture, close and glossy. (Heavier coats with undercoats permissible.) Coat placed well over body with ruff on neck preferred, and

more scanty on head and ears. Hair on tail preferred furry. In *Long Coats*, the coat should be of a soft texture, either flat or slightly wavy, with undercoat preferred. *Ears—*Fringed. *Tail—*Full and long (as a plume). Feathering on feet and legs, pants on hind legs and large ruff on the neck desired and preferred. (The Chihuahua should be groomed only to create a neat appearance.) *Disqualification—In Long Coats, too thin coat that resembles bareness.*

Color

Any color—Solid, marked or splashed.

Gait

The Chihuahua should move swiftly with a firm, sturdy action, with good reach in front equal to the drive from the rear. From the rear, the hocks remain parallel to each other, and the foot fall of the rear legs follows directly behind that of the forelegs. The legs, both front and rear, will tend to converge slightly toward a central line of gravity as speed increases. The side view shows good, strong drive in the rear and plenty of reach in the front, with head carried high. The topline should remain firm and the backline level as the dog moves.

Temperament

Alert, projecting the 'terrier-like' attitudes of self importance, confidence, self-reliance.

Disqualifications

Any dog over 6 pounds in weight.
Broken down or cropped ears.
Docked tail, bobtail.
In Long Coats, too thin coat that resembles bareness.

Approved August 12, 2008
Effective October 1, 2008

Useful Addresses and Literature

Organizations
The Chihuahua Club of America, Inc.
www.chihuahuaclubofamerica.com

American Kennel Club (AKC)
(919) 233-9767
www.akc.org

Canadian Kennel Club
(800) 250-8040
www.ckc.ca

United Kennel Club (UKC)
(616) 343-9020
www.ukcdogs.com

Home Again Microchip Service
1-800-HOME-AGAIN

Therapy Dogs International
(973) 252-9800
www.tdi-dog.org

United States Dog Agility Association (USDAA)
(972) 231-9700
www.usdaa.com

Rescue
Chihuahua Club of America Rescue Referral
www.chihuahuaclubofamerica.com

Pet Finder
www.petfinder.org

Periodicals
Top Notch Toys Magazine
www.topnotchtoys.com

Dog Fancy Magazine
www.dogchannel.com/dog-magazines/dogfancy/default.aspx

Books
Coile, D. Caroline. *Encyclopedia of Dog Breeds.* Hauppauge, NY: Barron's Educational Series, Inc., 2005.
____. *Show Me! A Dog Showing Primer.* Hauppauge, NY: Barron's Educational Series, Inc., 2009.
____. *The Chihuahua Handbook.* Hauppauge, NY: Barron's Educational Series, Inc., 2010.

Internet Sources
The Chihuahua Webring
www.webring.org/hub/chiring

Big Chihuahua Webpage and mailing list
www.bigchihuahua.com

Club Chihuahua
www.clubchi.com

AKC Canine Health Foundation
www.akcchf.org

Canine Health Information Center
www.caninehealthinfo.org

Photo Credits

Seth Casteel: pages 7, 8, 12, 14, 36 (bottom), 92. dreamstime.com: page 37. istock.com: pages 6, 20, 25. Paulette Johnson: page 60. Shutterstock.com: Alexia Khruscheva, page 9, 38 (bottom); AnetaPics, page 64; Anneka, page 30; Annette Shaff, page 40, 79; Christian Mueller, page 47; cynoclub, page 4, 14, 18, 22, 25, 29, 39, 43, 44, 50, 56, 57, 58, 73, 81, 91; Eric Isselee, page 11, 15, 36, 38 (top), 41, 45, 49, 53, 69, 70, 82, 83, 85, 86; Erik Lam, page 5, 68; iodrakon, page 77; Jagodka, page 21; John L. Smith, page 2; Julia Remezova, page 16; Karramba Production, page 62; Nadezha V. Kulagina, page 35, 66; Nikolai Pozdeev, page 13, 24, 48, 63, 74; Paul Michael Hughes, page 72; Scorpp, page 65; Steve Shoup, page 46; Susan Schmitz, page 33; Utekhina Anna, page 10, 13, 75; Vitaly Titov and Maria Sidelnikova, page 59, 80, 88. Connie Summers: pages 27, 54 (top and bottom), 55, 84. Joan Hustace Walker: pages 24 (top), 26, 31, 32.

Important Note

This pet owner's guide tells readers how to buy or adopt, and care for, a Chihuahua. The author and the publisher consider it important to point out that the advice given in this book is meant primarily for normally developed dogs of excellent physical health and good character.

Anyone who adopts a fully-grown dog should be aware that the animal has already formed its basic impression of human beings. The new owner should watch the animal carefully, including its behavior toward humans.

If the dog comes from a shelter, it may be possible to get some information on the dog's background and peculiarities there. There are dogs that, as the result of bad experiences with humans, behave in an unnatural manner or may even bite. Only people that have experience with dogs should take in such animals.

Caution is further advised in the association of children with dogs, in meeting other dogs, and in exercising the dog without a leash.

Even well-behaved and carefully supervised dogs sometimes do damage to someone else's property or cause accidents. It is therefore in the owner's interest to be adequately insured against such eventualities, and we strongly urge all dog owners to purchase a liability policy that covers their dog.

Cover Photos

Shutterstock.com: Julia Wolff, front cover; xtrekx, inside front cover; gillmar, inside back cover; cynoclub, back cover.

Acknowledgments

The author wishes to thank both the American Kennel Club and the Chihuahua Club of America for granting permission to reprint the official breed standard for the Chihuahua.

About the Author

D. Caroline Coile, Ph.D. has written 34 books and hundreds of articles about dogs. Among her books are *Barron's Encyclopedia of Dog Breeds* and *Show Me! A Dog Showing Primer*. Over the last 35 years her dogs have won top awards in conformation, obedience, agility, and field events. Caroline shares her office with her dogs, who lure her away from her work on a regular basis.

A Note on Pronouns

Many dog lovers feel that the pronoun "it" is not appropriate when referring to a beloved pet. For this reason, Chihuahuas are referred to as "she" throughout this book unless the topic specifically relates to male dogs. No gender bias is intended by this writing style.

All inquiries should be addressed to:
Barron's Educational Series, Inc.
250 Wireless Boulevard
Hauppauge, NY 11788
www.barronseduc.com

ISBN: 978-1-4380-0148-7

Library of Congress Control Number: 2012945315

Printed in China
9 8 7 6 5 4 3 2 1